PROVERBS FOR PROFIT
ANCIENT WISDOM FOR MODERN BUSINESS ETHICS

RICHARD FRENCH

Indie Pen Press

TURNING DREAMS INTO BESTSELLERS

Indie Pen Press
Gig Harbor WA 98332
IndiePenPress.com

First Edition

Paperback ISBN: 979-8-9917570-5-8

❀ Created with Vellum

ONE
THE FOUNDATION OF ETHICAL BUSINESS - INTEGRITY

"*T*he integrity of the upright guides them, but the unfaithful are destroyed by their duplicity.*" - Proverbs 11:3*

Sarah Smith, CEO of TechFusion Innovations stood at the floor-to-ceiling windows of her corner office, gazing out at the San Francisco skyline. The setting sun cast a golden glow across the city, but Sarah's mind whirled with the gravity of the decision before her.

TechFusion, a rising star in the artificial intelligence industry, teetered on the brink of a breakthrough. Their latest algorithm promised to revolutionize predictive analytics for financial markets. If successful, it would catapult the company into the upper echelons of the tech world, securing its position as a major player and likely quintupling its valuation.

One significant hurdle remained: the algorithm relied on a vast amount of user data, some of which TechFusion had collected without explicit consent. Sarah's team assured her the legal risks were minimal. "Everybody does it," her Chief Technology Officer had argued. "It's the cost of innovation."

But as Sarah stood there, her grandmother's words echoed in her mind. Grandmother Smith, a woman who had built a successful small business from nothing, often quoted proverbs to guide her granddaughter. Among them, one stood out:

"The integrity of the upright guides them, but the unfaithful are destroyed by their duplicity."

Sarah's hand clenched around her smartphone. One call could set the algorithm's in motion. Another could halt it indefinitely. The weight of the decision pressed down on her shoulders like a physical force.

Another proverb surfaced in her thoughts: "Whoever walks in integrity walks securely, but whoever takes crooked paths will be found out" (Proverbs 10:9). The path of integrity might be more arduous, but it offered a security that no amount of success built on deception could provide.

In boardrooms and offices worldwide, business leaders face similar crossroads daily. The pressure to succeed, innovate, and outpace competitors often clashes with ethical considerations. In these moments, integrity becomes more than a lofty ideal—it transforms into the bedrock upon which sustainable, ethical businesses are built.

DEFINING INTEGRITY IN BUSINESS

Integrity, derived from the Latin word "integer," meaning whole or complete, extends far beyond mere honesty. In a business context, integrity encompasses consistency of actions, values, methods, policies, principles, expectations, and outcomes. It demands alignment between what a company or individual says and what they do.

The proverb states, "The Lord detests dishonest scales, but accurate weights find favor with him" (Proverbs 11:1). This ancient wisdom underscores the importance of fairness and honesty in all business dealings.

For Sarah Smith and countless other business leaders, integrity manifests in monumental and mundane decisions. It shapes how a company treats employees, interacts with customers, deals with suppliers, and reports to shareholders. Integrity influences product quality, marketing strategies, and responses to crises.

Consider the following scenarios:

1. A software company discovers a security flaw in its flagship product. Fixing it will delay a major release and potentially cost millions in lost revenue. Should the company disclose the vulnerability and postpone the release, or should it push forward and address the issue in a later update?
2. A manufacturing firm receives a report of unsafe working conditions in one of its overseas factories. Addressing the issue will increase production costs and impact the company's competitiveness. How does the firm respond?
3. A pharmaceutical company develops a drug that shows promise in treating a rare disease. However, the potential market is small, and development costs are high. Should the company pursue the drug's development or allocate resources to more profitable ventures?

In each of these scenarios, the path of integrity may not align with short-term profitability or expediency. Yet, as we will explore, choosing integrity often leads to long-term success and sustainability. As another proverb wisely counsels, "Ill-gotten treasures have no lasting value, but righteousness delivers from death" (Proverbs 10:2).

THE BUSINESS CASE FOR INTEGRITY

Cynics might argue that integrity is a luxury businesses cannot afford in today's cutthroat global economy. They contend that "nice guys finish last" and ethical considerations hamper a company's ability to compete effectively. This perspective, however, needs to account for the numerous ways integrity contributes to long-term business success.

1. Trust and Reputation

In an age of instant communication and viral social media, a company's reputation can be its greatest asset —or its greatest liability. Businesses known for integrity enjoy more substantial relationships with customers, employees, and partners. This trust translates into customer loyalty, employee retention, and favorable terms with suppliers and creditors.

The outdoor clothing company Patagonia has built its brand on environmental stewardship and ethical business practices. Its "Don't Buy This Jacket" campaign, which encouraged consumers to consider the environmental impact of their purchases, paradoxically led to increased sales and customer loyalty. By aligning its actions with its stated values, Patagonia has cultivated a devoted customer base willing to pay premium prices for its products.

As the proverb states, "A good name is more desirable than great riches; to be esteemed is better than silver or gold" (Proverbs 22:1).

2. Employee Engagement and Productivity

Companies known for integrity attract and retain top talent. Employees who believe in their company's mission and trust its leadership exhibit higher levels of engagement, productivity, and innovation.

A study by the Great Place to Work Institute found that companies on Fortune's 100 Best Companies to Work For list, which includes the ethical treatment of employees as a key criterion, outperformed the S&P 500 by a factor of 3 between 1997 and 2013.

This aligns with the proverb, "The integrity of the upright guides them, but the unfaithful are destroyed by their duplicity" (Proverbs 11:3). Companies prioritizing integrity create an environment where employees can thrive and contribute their best work.

3. Risk Mitigation

Ethical lapses can result in severe financial and reputational damage. From regulatory fines to class-action lawsuits to consumer boycotts, the costs of unethical behavior often far outweigh any short-term gains.

The 2015 Volkswagen emissions scandal is a stark reminder of the risks of ethical breaches. The company's decision to install software to cheat emissions tests led to billions in fines, a massive recall, and incalculable damage to its brand. Years later, Volkswagen continues to grapple with the fallout from this ethical lapse.

As the proverb warns, "Whoever walks in integrity walks securely, but whoever takes crooked paths will be found out" (Proverbs 10:9).

4. Innovation and Adaptability

Companies with strong ethical foundations often exhibit more significant innovation and adaptability. By fostering a culture of openness and integrity, these organizations encourage employees to voice concerns, share ideas, and take calculated risks without fear of reprisal.

Google's former motto, "Don't be evil," (later changed to "Do the right thing") exemplified this approach. By prioritizing ethical considerations alongside innovation, Google created an environment where employees felt empowered to pursue groundbreaking projects while maintaining a strong moral compass.

This aligns with the proverb, "The way of the Lord is a refuge for the blameless, but it is the ruin of those who do evil" (Proverbs 10:29).

5. Sustainable Growth

Integrity provides a stable foundation for long-term growth. Companies built on ethical principles can weather economic downturns and industry disruptions more effectively than those relying on short-term tactics or unethical practices.

Johnson & Johnson's handling of the 1982 Tylenol crisis exemplifies this principle. When several people died after taking tainted Tylenol capsules, the company immediately recalled all Tylenol products nationwide, despite no evidence of tampering outside the Chicago area. This decisive action prioritized public safety over short-term profits, saved lives, and preserved consumer trust. Johnson & Johnson's stock price, which initially fell, rebounded within two months, and the company emerged from the crisis with its reputation enhanced.

As the proverb states, "Wealth from get-rich-quick schemes quickly disappears; wealth from hard work grows over time" (Proverbs 13:11, NLT).

THE CHALLENGES OF MAINTAINING INTEGRITY

While the benefits of integrity in business are evident, maintaining ethical standards in the face of complex challenges can prove daunting. Business leaders often grapple with competing priorities, ambiguous situations, and pressure from various stakeholders.

1. Short-term Pressure vs. Long-term Vision

The demand for quarterly results and constant growth can tempt leaders to compromise ethical standards for immediate gains. Resisting this pressure requires a solid commitment to long-term sustainability and a clear understanding of how integrity contributes to lasting success.

As the proverb cautions, "Dishonest money dwindles away, but whoever gathers money little by little makes it grow" (Proverbs 13:11).

2. Cultural Differences

Companies must navigate varying cultural norms and ethical standards in a globalized business environment. Practices considered acceptable in one country may be viewed as unethical in another. Leaders must develop a nuanced understanding of cultural differences while maintaining core ethical principles.

The proverb reminds us, "The righteous detest the dishonest; the wicked detest the upright" (Proverbs 29:27). Maintaining integrity across diverse cultural contexts requires wisdom and discernment.

3. Technological Advancements

Rapid technological progress often outpaces ethical frameworks and regulations. Companies at the forefront of innovation, like those in AI, biotechnology, or data analytics, must grapple with unprecedented ethical questions.

As the proverb states, "The simple believe anything, but the prudent give thought to their steps" (Proverbs 14:15). Leaders must carefully consider the ethical implications of new technologies.

4. Competitive Pressure

When competitors engage in unethical practices without apparent consequences, the temptation to "level the playing field" by lowering ethical standards can be substantial. Maintaining integrity in such environments requires courage and a long-term perspective.

The proverb reminds us, "Better a little with righteousness than much gain with injustice" (Proverbs 16:8).

5. Ethical Dilemmas

Not all ethical decisions are clear-cut. Leaders often face situations where multiple ethical principles conflict, requiring careful consideration and sometimes tricky trade-offs.

As the proverb advises, "The wise in heart accept commands, but a chattering fool comes to ruin" (Proverbs 10:8). Seeking wise counsel and carefully considering ethical implications are crucial in navigating complex dilemmas.

BUILDING A CULTURE OF INTEGRITY

Creating and maintaining an organization's integrity culture requires deliberate effort and ongoing commitment. Here are critical strategies for fostering integrity:

1. Lead by Example

Integrity must start at the top. Leaders should consistently demonstrate ethical behavior in their decisions and actions. When faced with ethical dilemmas, leaders should openly discuss the decision-making process, reinforcing the importance of integrity throughout the organization.

As the proverb states, "Whoever walks in integrity walks securely, but whoever takes crooked paths will be found out" (Proverbs 10:9).

2. Clear Communication of Values

Organizations should clearly articulate their ethical standards and values. These principles should be integrated into mission statements, employee handbooks, and regular communications. More importantly, they should be reflected in day-to-day operations and decision-making processes.

The proverb reminds us, "The tongue that brings healing is a tree of life, but a deceitful tongue crushes the spirit" (Proverbs 15:4).

3. Ethics Training and Education

Regular ethics training helps employees recognize ethical issues and provides them with tools to navigate complex situations. This training should go beyond compliance to foster a deep understanding of the company's values and the importance of ethical decision-making.

As the proverb advises, "Apply your heart to instruction and your ears to words of knowledge" (Proverbs 23:12).

4. Encourage Open Communication

Create an environment where employees feel safe raising concerns and reporting potential ethical breaches without fear of retaliation. Implement robust whistleblower protection policies and anonymous reporting mechanisms.

The proverb states, "The way of fools seems right to them, but the wise listen to advice" (Proverbs 12:15).

5. Accountability and Consequences

Establish clear consequences for ethical violations, regardless of an individual's position within the company. Conversely, recognize and reward ethical behavior and decisions prioritizing integrity over short-term gains.

As the proverb warns, "One who has no rule over his own spirit is like a city broken down, without walls" (Proverbs 25:28, NKJV).

6. Regular Ethical Audits

Conduct regular assessments of the organization's ethical climate. This can include employee surveys, reviews of decision-making processes, and evaluations of how well the company's actions align with its stated values.

The proverb reminds us, "The crucible for silver and the furnace for gold, but the Lord tests the heart" (Proverbs 17:3).

7. Ethical Considerations in Strategic Planning

Integrate ethical considerations into strategic planning processes. When evaluating new initiatives or responding to challenges, explicitly consider the ethical implications alongside financial and operational factors.

As the proverb states, "Commit to the Lord whatever you do, and he will establish your plans" (Proverbs 16:3).

THE PATH FORWARD

As Sarah Smith stood in her office, weighing the decision before her, she reflected on the journey that had brought her to this moment. TechFusion had grown from a small startup to a significant player in the tech industry, primarily due to its reputation for innovation and ethical practices.

The algorithm in question promised unprecedented accuracy in financial predictions. It could revolutionize investment strategies, potentially democratizing access to sophisticated financial tools. But at what cost? The use of data collected without explicit consent violated the very principles of transparency and respect for user privacy that TechFusion had championed.

Sarah's grandmother's words echoed once more: "The integrity of the upright guides them, but the unfaithful are destroyed by their duplicity."

With a deep breath, Sarah made her decision. She picked up her phone and dialed her Chief Technology Officer.

"Jack, it's Sarah. I've decided on the algorithm. We're not going to release it—not in its current form. I want a full review of our data collection practices, and I want us to explore ways to achieve similar results with only explicitly consented data. It may delay our release, but it's the right thing to do."

There was a pause on the other end of the line. Then, Jack's voice came through, tinged with respect and relief. "I understand, Sarah. I've been wrestling with this myself. I think you're making the right call."

As Sarah ended the call, she felt a weight lift from her shoulders. The path ahead would be challenging. Competitors might leap ahead while TechFusion recalibrates its approach. Investors might grumble about missed opportunities. But Sarah knew in her heart she had chosen the path of integrity— the only path that would lead to sustainable, ethical success.

She recalled another proverb her grandmother often quoted: "The highway of the upright avoids evil; those who guard their ways preserve their lives" (Proverbs 16:17). By choosing the path of integrity, Sarah was not only preserving TechFusion's reputation but also setting a course for long-term success and fulfillment.

In boardrooms and offices worldwide, countless leaders face similar decisions daily. The pressure to succeed, innovate, and outpace competitors often clashes with ethical considerations. In these moments, integrity becomes more than a lofty ideal—it transforms into the bedrock upon which sustainable, ethical businesses are built.

As we navigate the complex landscape of modern business, let us remember the wisdom encapsulated in Proverbs 11:3. Let integrity be our guide, steering us toward decisions that drive success and contribute to a more ethical, sustainable business world.

In the following chapters, we will explore further how the timeless wisdom of Proverbs can illuminate our path through the ethical challenges of contemporary business. From fair dealing and wise leadership to the perils of greed and the value of a good name, we will uncover how ancient insights can guide us in building businesses that profit and contribute positively to our world.

The journey of ethical business can be challenging, but it is always worthwhile. As we will see, those who choose the path of integrity often find it leads to sustainable success and a more profound, fulfilling experience of business and life.

Let us move forward, guided by the wisdom of the ages, as we explore the rich intersection of ancient principles and modern business practices.

TWO
FAIR DEALING - THE CORNERSTONE OF SUSTAINABLE BUSINESS

"*H*onest scales and balances belong to the Lord; all the weights in the bag are of his making." - Proverbs 16:11

The factory floor buzzed with activity. Conveyor belts whirred, carrying components destined for assembly into high-end smartphones. Mark Thompson, CEO of Nexus Electronics, walked the line, his keen eyes searching for inefficiencies, his mind racing with possibilities.

Nexus had grown from a small contract manufacturer to a major player in the electronics industry. They were at a crossroads, about to launch their own line of smartphones.

A ping from Mark's smartwatch caught his attention. An alert from the supply chain management system. He frowned and tapped the screen to display the entire message. Their primary supplier of rare earth metals had raised prices again, citing increased mining costs and environmental regulations.

Mark's jaw clenched. The timing couldn't be worse. With the launch of their flagship phone just months away, any increase in production costs threatened to erode their already thin margins. The pressure to cut corners and find a way to maintain profitability increased with every passing second.

As he walked back to his office, the voice of Mark's grandfather echoed in his mind. The older man had built a modest but respected hardware store from nothing, weathering economic downturns and big-box competition with an unwavering commitment to fair dealing. "Remember, Mark," he'd say, quoting his favorite proverb, "Honest scales and balances belong to the Lord; all the weights in the bag are of his making."

Another proverb surfaced in Mark's thoughts: "Better a little with righteousness than much gain with injustice" (Proverbs 16:8). The path of fair dealing might be more complex. Yet it offered a security that no success based on deception could provide.

Mark sank into his chair, the weight of the decision before him pressing down on him like a physical force. In a world of razor-thin margins and cutthroat competition, could a business truly thrive while adhering to the principles of fair dealing? Or was his grandfather's wisdom a relic of a bygone era, ill-suited to the realities of modern global commerce?

THE ESSENCE OF FAIR DEALING IN BUSINESS

At its core, Fair Dealing embodies the principle of conducting business with honesty, transparency and respect for all stakeholders. It goes beyond mere compliance with the law and includes a moral imperative to treat customers, employees, suppliers and competitors equally and fairly.

As the proverb states, "Differing weights and differing measures—the Lord detests them both" (Proverbs 20:10). This ancient wisdom underscores the importance of consistency and honesty in all business transactions.

In the context of modern business, fair dealing manifests in various ways:

1. **Pricing and Value**: Offer products or services at prices commensurate with their value, without exploiting information asymmetries or temporary market advantages.
2. **Transparent Communication**: Provide clear, accurate information about products, services and business practices to all stakeholders.
3. **Equitable Employment Practices**: Ensure fair compensation, safe working conditions, and opportunities for growth for all employees.
4. **Responsible Sourcing**: Maintain ethical supply chains, considering the costs and environmental and social impacts of sourcing decisions.
5. **Fair Competition**: Compete vigorously but ethically, without resorting to deceptive practices or unfair tactics to gain market advantage.
6. **Contractual Integrity**: Honor agreements and commitments, even when changing circumstances make them less advantageous.

The principle of fair dealing challenges companies to look beyond short-term gains and consider the broader, long-term implications of their actions. It requires a commitment to building lasting relationships and a reputation for trustworthiness.

As another proverb wisely counsels, "The Lord detests dishonest scales, but accurate weights find favor with him" (Proverbs 11:1).

THE BUSINESS CASE FOR FAIR DEALING

Skeptics may argue that fairness is a luxury in today's hyper-competitive business environment. They claim that cutthroat tactics and "creative" accounting are the only way to succeed. This perspective fails to recognize the many ways in which fair dealing contributes to long-term business success and sustainability.

1. Trust and Brand Loyalty

In the age of instant information and social media, a company's reputation for fairness can become its most valuable asset. Customers who trust a brand remain loyal, even in the face of competitive offers or economic downturns.

Consider the case of Costco. The retail giant's commitment to fair dealing, manifested in its treatment of employees, pricing strategies, and return policies, has cultivated fierce customer loyalty. Despite charging membership fees and operating on razor-thin margins, Costco has thrived and outperformed many of its competitors over the long term.

As the proverb states, "A good name is more desirable

than great riches; to be esteemed is better than silver or gold" (Proverbs 22:1).

2. Employee Engagement and Productivity

Companies with a reputation for fairness attract and retain top talent. Employees who believe they are treated fairly and work for an ethical company exhibit higher levels of engagement, productivity, and innovation.

Patagonia, the outdoor clothing company, exemplifies this principle. Its commitment to environmental sustainability and fair labor practices has created a highly engaged workforce. The company reports turnover rates well below industry averages, reducing recruitment and training costs while fostering a culture of innovation and commitment.

This aligns with the proverb, "Those who trust in their riches will fall, but the righteous will thrive like a green leaf" (Proverbs 11:28).

3. Supplier Relationships and Supply Chain Resilience

Dealing fairly with suppliers builds robust and resilient supply chains. Suppliers who trust their business partners are more likely to prioritize their needs, offer favorable terms, and work together to solve problems.

Toyota's approach to supplier relationships illustrates this benefit. The automaker's commitment to fair treatment and long-term partnerships has resulted in a highly efficient, innovative supply chain. In times of crisis, such as the 2011 Tōhoku earthquake and tsunami, Toyota's strong supplier relationships enabled it to recover faster than many competitors.

As the proverb advises, "Do not exploit the poor because they are poor and do not crush the needy in court, for the Lord will take up their case and will exact life for life" (Proverbs 22:22-23).

4. Regulatory Compliance and Risk Mitigation

A commitment to fair dealing often puts companies ahead of the regulatory curve, reducing the risk of fines, lawsuits, and reputational damage. It also builds goodwill with regulators and communities, potentially leading to more favorable treatment when problems arise.

Johnson & Johnson's handling of the 1982 Tylenol crisis, discussed in the previous chapter, exemplifies this principle. The company's swift, transparent response, which put public safety ahead of short-term profits, not only saved lives but also preserved consumer confidence and strengthened its relationship with regulators.

The proverb reminds us, "Whoever pursues righteousness and love finds life, prosperity and honor" (Proverbs 21:21).

5. Sustainable Growth and Long-term Profitability

While fair dealing may sometimes require sacrificing short-term gains, it often leads to more sustainable, profitable growth in the long run. Companies built on the principles of fair dealing can weather economic downturns and industry disruptions more effectively than those that rely on short-term tactics or unethical practices.

Warren Buffett's Berkshire Hathaway is a compelling example. Buffett's commitment to ethical business practices and fair dealing is a cornerstone of his investment philosophy. Over the decades, this approach has produced extraordinary returns that have significantly outperformed the broader market.

As the proverb states, "Dishonest money dwindles away, but whoever gathers money little by little makes it grow" (Proverbs 13:11).

CHALLENGES TO FAIR DEALING IN MODERN BUSINESS

While the benefits of doing business fairly are clear, upholding these standards in the face of complex business challenges can prove daunting. Business leaders often struggle with competing pressures and ethical dilemmas:

1. Global Supply Chains and Labor Practices

As supply chains expand globally, ensuring fair labor practices and environmental standards becomes increasingly complex. Companies must balance cost considerations with ethical sourcing, often in regions with vastly different regulatory environments and cultural norms.

The proverb cautions, "Do not exploit the poor because they are poor and do not crush the needy in court, for the Lord will take up their case and will exact life for life" (Proverbs 22:22-23).

2. Data Privacy and Digital Ethics

The digital age has brought unprecedented challenges to privacy and the ethical use of information. Companies must navigate complex issues around data collection, user consent, and algorithmic decision-making.

As the proverb advises, "The simple believe anything, but the prudent give thought to their steps" (Proverbs 14:15).

3. Short-term Pressures vs. Long-term Sustainability

The demand for quarterly results and constant growth can tempt leaders to compromise fairness for immediate gain. Resisting these pressures requires a solid commitment to long-term sustainability and clear communication with stakeholders.

The proverb reminds us, "The plans of the diligent lead to profit as surely as haste leads to poverty" (Proverbs 21:5).

4. Competitive Pressures and Industry Norms

In industries where unfair or deceptive practices have become the norm, companies committed to fair dealing may find themselves at a short-term competitive disadvantage. Overcoming this challenge requires courage, innovation, and effective stakeholder communication.

As the proverb states, "Better a little with righteousness than much gain with injustice" (Proverbs 16:8).

5. Balancing Stakeholder Interests

Acting fairly often requires balancing the interests of multiple stakeholders - customers, employees, shareholders, suppliers and communities. These interests can sometimes conflict, requiring careful consideration and sometimes difficult trade-offs.

The proverb advises, "The righteous care about justice for the poor, but the wicked have no such concern" (Proverbs 29:7).

STRATEGIES FOR IMPLEMENTING FAIR DEALING

Creating and maintaining a culture of fair dealing within an organization requires deliberate effort and ongoing commitment. Here are key strategies for promoting fair dealing:

1. Lead by Example

Fairness must start at the top. Leaders should consistently demonstrate a commitment to fairness in their decisions and actions. When faced with ethical dilemmas, leaders should openly discuss the decision-making process and reinforce the importance of fairness throughout the organization.

As the proverb states, "Kings detest wrongdoing, for a throne is established through righteousness" (Proverbs 16:12).

2. Develop Clear Policies and Guidelines

Organizations should establish clear policies on fair dealing. These policies should cover areas such as pricing strategies, supplier relationships, employee treatment, and competitive practices. More importantly, they should be consistently applied and regularly reviewed.

The proverb reminds us, "The path of the righteous is like the morning sun, shining ever brighter till the full light of day" (Proverbs 4:18).

3. Foster Transparency

Foster a culture of openness and transparency. This includes clear customer communication about products and services, transparent reporting to shareholders, and open dialogue with employees about business decisions and challenges.

As the proverb advises, "Whoever conceals their sins does not prosper, but the one who confesses and renounces them finds mercy" (Proverbs 28:13).

4. Invest in Ethical Supply Chains

Develop robust supplier verification and monitoring processes. This may include regular audits, supplier capacity-building programs, and collaborative initiatives to address industry-wide challenges.

The proverb states, "The righteous care about justice for the poor, but the wicked have no such concern" (Proverbs 29:7).

5. Prioritize Employee Well-being

Implement fair compensation practices, invest in employee development, and create a safe, inclusive work environment. Consider implementing profit-sharing or employee ownership programs to align employee interests with company success.

As the proverb counsels, "Those who oppress the poor to increase their wealth and those who give gifts to the rich—both come to poverty" (Proverbs 22:16).

6. Engage in Fair Competition

Compete vigorously but ethically. Avoid deceptive marketing practices, respect intellectual property rights, and refrain from anti-competitive behavior. Focus on creating value for customers, not undermining competitors.

The proverb reminds us, "Do not move an ancient

boundary stone or encroach on the fields of the father-less" (Proverbs 23:10).

7. Implement Ethical Decision-making Frameworks

Develop frameworks to help employees navigate complex ethical decisions. This may include ethics committees, decision trees, or guiding questions to ensure that fair dealing considerations are applied consistently.

As the proverb states, "Plans fail for lack of counsel, but with many advisers they succeed" (Proverbs 15:22).

8. Regular Training and Reinforcement

Provide ongoing training on the principles of fair dealing and their practical application. Recognize and reward behaviors that exemplify fair dealing to rein-force its importance.

The proverb advises, "Apply your heart to instruction and your ears to words of knowledge" (Proverbs 23:12).

THE PATH FORWARD

Mark Thompson leaned back in his chair, his mind racing with possibilities. The challenge before him was daunting, but possible. His grandfather echoed once more: "Honest scales and balances belong to the Lord; all the weights in the bag are of his making."

With renewed determination, Mark began to formulate a plan. Instead of looking for ways to cut corners or squeeze suppliers, he would look for ways to innovate - to create more value for customers while maintaining their commitment to fair dealing.

He drafted an email to his executive team calling for an emergency strategy session. They would explore options for vertical integration in their supply chain and invest in recycling technologies to reduce their dependence on raw materials. They would redouble their research and development efforts, seeking breakthroughs in energy efficiency and durability to differentiate their products in the marketplace.

It wouldn't be an easy path of fair dealing rarely was Mark knew in his heart that it was the only sustainable way forward. By staying true to its principles, Nexus could build something truly lasting - a company that was not only profitable but worthy of the trust placed in it by customers, employees, and partners alike.

As he finalized his notes, another proverb came to mind: "The integrity of the upright guides them, but the unfaithful are destroyed by their duplicity" (Proverbs 11:3). By choosing the path of fair dealing, Mark not only preserved Nexus's reputation, but also set the stage for long-term success and fulfillment.

As business leaders navigate the complex landscape of modern commerce, the principle of fair dealing serves as a compass, guiding decisions toward long-term sustainability and success. It challenges us to look beyond short-term gains and consider the broader implications of our actions.

The wisdom encapsulated in Proverbs 16:11 remains as relevant today as it was millennia ago. In a world of "creative accounting" and "growth hacking," the commitment to honest scales and balances stands out as a beacon of integrity.

As we explore ancient wisdom in modern business, let us carry this principle of fair dealing with us. In future chapters, we will explore related themes- the dangers of greed, the value of a good name, and the importance of ethical leadership. Fair dealing will remain a foundation upon which sustainable, ethical businesses can be built.

The journey of ethical business is rarely easy, but it is always worthwhile. As we will see, those who choose the path of fair dealing often find that it leads to lasting success and a deeper, more fulfilling experience of business and life.

Let us move forward, guided by the principle of fair dealing, as we continue to explore the rich intersection of ancient principles and modern business practices.

THREE
THE PERIL OF GREED - BALANCING PROFIT AND ETHICS

" *A greedy man brings trouble to his family, but the one who hates bribes will live.*" - *Proverbs 15:27*

The sleek boardroom at Apex Pharmaceuticals buzzed with anticipation. Emma Reeves, newly appointed CEO, stood at the head of the polished mahogany table, her piercing gaze sweeping the faces of her executive team. The air crackled with tension as she prepared to unveil the company's strategy for the coming year.

"Ladies and gentlemen," Emma began, her voice calm and controlled, "we are at a crossroads. Our shareholders are demanding growth. The marketplace expects innovation. Our competitors are breathing down our necks." She paused, letting the weight of her words sink in. "And I intend to deliver on all fronts."

A chorus of agreement rippled through the room. Emma allowed herself a small smile before continuing. "Our R&D

team has developed a promising new drug to treat chronic pain. Initial trials show efficacy rates that far exceed anything currently on the market."

The Chief Scientific Officer, Dr. Alan Patel, nodded in agreement, a gleam of pride in his eyes.

"However," Emma continued, her tone sharpening, "the FDA approval process could take years. Years we don't have if we want to maintain our market position and meet shareholder expectations."

The room fell silent. Emma could almost hear the gears turning in the heads of her executives as they grappled with the implications of her words.

"I propose we fast-track this drug to market. We'll conduct abbreviated trials in countries with... let's say, more flexible regulatory environments. We'll leverage our connections to expedite approvals. And we'll launch an aggressive marketing campaign to establish market dominance before our competitors can catch up."

The silence stretched, tight as a bowstring. Then, one by one, heads began to nod. Murmurs of agreement turned into enthusiastic discussions of possible strategies.

Only Dr. Patel remained silent, his brow furrowed in concern. "Emma," he began, his voice barely above a whisper, "what about the potential long-term side effects that we haven't had time to study? What if..."

Emma cut him off with a sharp glance. "Alan, I appreciate your concern for safety. But in this industry, he who hesitates is lost. We can't afford to be left behind. The potential rewards far outweigh the risks."

As the meeting adjourned and the executives filed out, their excited chatter filling the air, Emma felt a surge of adrenaline. This was her moment, her chance to prove herself and cement Apex's position at the top of the industry.

But as she gathered her papers, a nagging voice echoed in the back of her mind. The voice of her mentor, the former CEO, quoting an old proverb during her final days of training: "A greedy man brings trouble to his family, but the one who hates bribes will live."

Emma shook her head, dismissing the thought. This wasn't greed, she told herself. This was business. This was progress. This was necessary.

Wasn't it?

Another proverb flickered through her mind, one she had often heard in her business ethics class: "Better a little with righteousness than much gain with injustice." (Proverbs 16:8) Emma pushed the thought aside. They weren't being unjust, she reasoned. They were simply being... efficient.

THE NATURE OF GREED IN BUSINESS

At its core, greed is an insatiable desire for more-more money, more power, more market share, more success. In the business world, it often manifests itself as a relentless pursuit of profit at the expense of ethical considerations, long-term sustainability, and the well-being of stakeholders.

The line between healthy ambition and destructive greed can be a fine one. Ambition drives innovation, fuels growth, and pushes companies to create value for customers and society. Greed, on the other hand, prioritizes short-term gain over long-term sustainability, often leading to unethical practices and ultimately self-destruction.

As the ancient proverb warns, "The wealth of the rich is their fortified city; they imagine it a wall too high to scale." (Proverbs 18:11) This false sense of security often leads to reckless decision-making and ethical compromises.

In the modern business landscape, greed can take many forms:

1. **Profit Maximization at All Costs**: Prioritizing shareholder returns above all else, even at the expense of employee well-being, customer safety, or environmental sustainability.
2. **Market Domination**: Seeking to crush competition through predatory pricing, patent hoarding, or other anti-competitive practices, rather than focusing on innovation and value creation.
3. **Executive Compensation**: Excessive executive pay packages disconnected from company performance or employee wages.
4. **Short-term Thinking**: Focusing on quarterly results and short-term stock price fluctuations at the expense of long-term company health and sustainability.
5. **Regulatory Evasion**: Exploiting loopholes, lobbying for favorable treatment, or outright violating regulations to increase profits.
6. **Exploitation**: Taking advantage of information asymmetry, market inefficiencies, or vulnerable populations for financial gain.

The siren call of greed can be particularly seductive in high-pressure business environments where success is often measured solely in financial terms. However, as we will explore, giving in to this temptation often leads to disastrous consequences, both for the individuals involved and for their organizations.

THE DESTRUCTIVE POWER OF GREED

History is replete with cautionary tales of greed in business. From the collapse of Enron to the 2008 financial crisis, the consequences of unchecked greed have been far-reaching and devastating. Let's examine some notable examples:

1. Enron: The Perils of Financial Deception

Enron's downfall is a stark reminder of how greed can corrupt even the most promising companies. Once hailed as America's most innovative company, Enron's executives engaged in a complex web of financial deception to inflate profits and hide debt. Their greed not only destroyed the company, but also wiped out thousands of jobs and billions in pension funds.

The lesson: Greed-driven financial manipulation may create the illusion of short-term success, but it inevitably leads to catastrophic failure.. As the proverb states, "A fortune made by a lying tongue is a fleeting vapor and a deadly snare." (Proverbs 21:6)

2. Volkswagen: The Emissions Scandal

Volkswagen's decision to install software to cheat emissions tests on its diesel vehicles illustrates how greed can drive even established companies to brazen deception. The company's desire to dominate the auto-

motive market led it to put sales ahead of environmental regulations and customer trust. The
consequences were severe: billions in fines, criminal
charges against executives, and incalculable damage to
the brand's reputation. Years later, Volkswagen
continues to grapple with the fallout from its ethical
lapse.

The lesson: Greed-driven shortcuts and deception may
provide a temporary market advantage, but they can
lead to long-term financial and reputational damage.

3. Theranos: The Danger of Hype Over Substance

The rise and fall of Theranos illustrates how greed can
fuel a culture of deception and willful ignorance.
Founder Elizabeth Holmes, driven by a desire for
wealth and acclaim, made grandiose claims about the
company's blood-testing technology. Despite
mounting evidence that the technology didn't work as
claimed, Holmes continued to seek investment and put
patients at risk. The company's eventual exposure led
to its dissolution, criminal charges against its leaders,
and a cautionary tale for the entire startup ecosystem.

The lesson: Greed can blind leaders to reality, causing
them to prioritize hype and personal gain over true
innovation and customer welfare.

4. The 2008 Financial Crisis: Systemic Greed

The 2008 financial crisis showed how greed could
infect entire industries and threaten the global econ-

omy. Financial institutions, driven by an insatiable appetite for profits, engaged in increasingly risky behavior, from predatory lending to the creation of complex financial instruments they barely understood. The resulting meltdown led to millions of job losses, home foreclosures, and a global economic downturn that took years to recover from.

The lesson: When greed becomes systemic, its destructive power can extend far beyond individual companies to affect entire economies and societies. These examples illustrate a common thread: greed-driven decisions may yield short-term gains, but they invariably lead to long-term destruction. They erode trust, stifle true innovation, and ultimately destroy rather than create value.. As another proverb wisely counsels, "Do not wear yourself out to get rich; do not trust your own cleverness." (Proverbs 23:4)

THE BUSINESS CASE AGAINST GREED

While the destructive power of greed is clear, it's equally important to recognize that resisting greed is not only a moral imperative - it's a sound business strategy. Companies that prioritize ethical practices and long-term value creation over short-term greed often outperform their less scrupulous counterparts in the long run.

1. **Trust and Brand Value:** In an age of transparency and instant communication, a company's reputation is one of its most valuable assets. Ethical companies build trust with customers, employees, and partners, leading to stronger brand loyalty and resilience in

times of crisis. Consider the case of Patagonia, the outdoor clothing company. Patagonia has built a fiercely loyal customer base and brand value far beyond its size by prioritizing environmental sustainability and ethical practices over the bottom line.

2. **Employee Engagement and Talent Retention:** Companies known for ethical practices attract and retain top talent more effectively than those perceived as greedy or unethical. Engaged employees are more productive, more innovative and more likely to go the extra mile for the company and its customers. Costco's approach to employee compensation and benefits exemplifies this principle. By paying higher wages and providing better benefits than many of its competitors, Costco has achieved lower turnover and higher productivity, contributing to its long-term success.

3. **Innovation and Adaptability:** A focus on short-term profits often leads companies to prioritize incremental improvements and cost reductions over true innovation. In contrast, companies that resist greed in favor of long-term value creation are more likely to invest in transformative innovations that create new markets and drive sustainable growth. Apple, under the leadership of Steve Jobs, demonstrated this principle. By focusing on creating revolutionary products rather than maximizing short-term profits, Apple transformed itself from a niche computer maker into one of the world's most valuable companies.

4. **Regulatory Compliance and Risk Management:** Ethical companies that prioritize

compliance and responsible practices face lower regulatory risks and are better positioned to adapt to changing regulations. This approach not only reduces the risk of fines and legal challenges, but also builds goodwill with regulators and the public. Johnson & Johnson's handling of the 1982 Tylenol crisis, discussed in earlier chapters, illustrates how a commitment to ethical practices can help a company weather crises and emerge stronger.

5. **Sustainable Growth and Long-term Profitability:** While resisting greed may sometimes mean sacrificing short-term profits, it often leads to more sustainable, profitable growth in the long run. Companies built on ethical foundations are better equipped to weather economic downturns and industry disruptions. Warren Buffett's Berkshire Hathaway provides a compelling example of how a long-term, ethical approach to business can yield extraordinary returns. Buffett's focus on investing in companies with strong ethical foundations has resulted in consistent outperformance of the broader market for decades. This approach embodies the wisdom of the proverb, "Whoever trusts in his riches will fall, but the righteous will thrive like a green leaf." (Proverbs 11:28)

STRATEGIES FOR BALANCING PROFIT AND ETHICS

Recognizing the dangers of greed is one thing; actively cultivating a culture that balances the pursuit of profit with ethical considerations is another. Here are key strategies for business leaders seeking to achieve this critical balance:

1. **Define and Communicate Clear Ethical Standards:** Develop a comprehensive code of ethics that goes beyond mere legal compliance. Ensure these standards are clearly communicated throughout the organization and integrated into decision-making processes at all levels.

2. **Align Incentives with Ethical Behavior:** Redesign compensation and promotion structures to reward long-term value creation and ethical behavior rather than short-term profit maximization. Consider including ethical metrics in performance evaluations.

3. **Foster a Culture of Transparency:** Encourage open communication about ethical challenges and dilemmas. Create safe channels for employees to raise concerns without fear of retaliation. Leaders should model transparency by openly discussing the ethical implications of important decisions.

4. **Invest in Ethics Training:** Provide ongoing ethics training for all employees, with an emphasis on practical application to day-to-day decision-making. Use case studies and role-playing exercises to help employees navigate complex ethical situations.

5. **Prioritize Stakeholder Value:** Expand the definition of success beyond shareholder returns to include value creation for all stakeholders-employees, customers, suppliers, communities, and the environment. Regularly assess and report on the company's impact on these stakeholders.

6. **Implement Ethical Decision-Making Frameworks:** Develop frameworks to help employees navigate complex ethical decisions. This could include ethics committees, decision trees, or guiding

questions to ensure that ethical considerations are applied consistently.

7. **Cultivate Long-term Thinking:** Resist the tyranny of quarterly earnings by setting and communicating long-term goals. Invest in initiatives that may not yield immediate returns but contribute to long-term sustainability and value creation.

8. **Lead by Example:** Leaders must consistently demonstrate ethical behavior, especially when there is a personal or short-term cost. Their actions set the tone for the entire organization.

9. **Embrace Moderation:** Recognize that sustainable success doesn't require extreme measures or excessive risk-taking. As the proverb suggests, "Better a little with righteousness than much gain with injustice." (Proverbs 16:8) Focus on steady, ethical growth rather than explosive but potentially unsustainable expansion.

THE PATH FORWARD

As the sun dipped below the horizon, casting long shadows across her office, Emma Reeves sat alone, her former bravado replaced by a gnawing uncertainty. The excited chatter of her executive team still echoed in her mind, but so did Dr. Patel's concerns-and the adage her mentor had shared.

She pulled up the latest trial data on her tablet, forcing herself to confront the numbers she'd previously glossed over. The potential side effects, while rare, were serious. The long-term effects remained unknown.

Emma's finger hovered over the "approve" button for the fast-track plan. One click and they'd be on their way to market dominance, skyrocketing stock prices, and personal accolades. Everything she'd worked her entire career for.

But at what cost?

Taking a deep breath, Emma closed the approval form and opened a new document. "Proposal for Comprehensive Safety Study," she typed, her fingers flying across the keyboard as a new plan took shape. It would take longer. It would cost more. Shareholders might grumble.

But it was the right thing to do.

As she worked late into the night, Emma felt a weight lift from her shoulders. She realized that true leadership wasn't about chasing short-term gains at any cost. It was about creating lasting value-for the company, for the patients it served, and for society as a whole.

In boardrooms and offices around the world, countless executives face similar decisions every day. The pressure to deliver results, outperform competitors, and meet or exceed market expectations can be overwhelming. In these moments, the temptation of greed-to cut corners, to put profits before people, to sacrifice long-term sustainability for short-term gain-can be almost irresistible.

But as we've explored in this chapter, giving in to that temptation often has disastrous consequences. From individual careers ruined to businesses collapsed to entire economies shaken, the destructive power of greed in business is well documented.

More importantly, we've seen that resisting greed is not only a moral imperative - it's a sound business strategy. Companies that prioritize ethical practices, long-term value creation, and the well-being of all stakeholders often outperform their less scrupulous counterparts over the long term.

As we continue our exploration of ancient wisdom in modern business, let the proverb that opened this chapter guide us: "A greedy man brings trouble to his family, but the one who hates bribes will live." In the complex landscape of modern business, this timeless wisdom reminds us to look beyond short-term gains and consider the broader, long-term implications of our actions.

In the chapters that follow, we will explore related themes-the power of ethical leadership, the value of a good name, and the importance of sustainable business practices. Throughout, the lessons learned about the perils of greed will serve as a foundation, a constant reminder of the importance of balancing the pursuit of profit with ethical considerations.

The path of ethical business is rarely the easiest. It often requires difficult decisions, short-term sacrifices, and the courage to stand firm in the face of pressure. But as we've seen, it's a path that leads not only to lasting success, but also to a deeper, more fulfilling experience of business and life.

Let us move forward, guided by the wisdom of the ages, as we continue to explore the rich intersection of ancient principles and modern business practices. In doing so, we can build businesses that not only make a profit, but also make a positive contribution to our world - creating value far beyond the balance sheet.

FOUR
WISE LEADERSHIP - THE POWER OF ETHICAL DECISION-MAKING

"*P lans fail for lack of counsel, but with many advisers, they succeed.*" - *Proverbs 15:22*

The tension in the room was palpable as Michael Rodriguez, CEO of GreenTech Solutions, faced his board of directors. The company, a pioneer in sustainable energy technologies, was at a crossroads. Its revolutionary solar panel design promised to double the efficiency of current models, potentially reshaping the entire renewable energy landscape.

But there was a catch.

"Gentlemen, ladies," Michael began, his voice steady despite the butterflies in his stomach, "we have made incredible progress with our new solar technology. The potential impact on global energy consumption is... frankly, staggering."

Nods of agreement rippled around the table. Pride gleamed in the eyes of the board members. GreenTech had always pushed the envelope, but this could be their legacy.

Michael took a deep breath before continuing. "However, our latest stress tests have revealed a potential weakness. Under extreme weather conditions - conditions we're seeing more frequently due to climate change - the panels could degrade more quickly than we originally predicted."

The room fell silent. Michael could almost hear the gears turning in the minds of his board members as they processed this information.

"What are our options?" asked Sandra Chen, head of the finance committee.

Michael squared his shoulders. "We have two paths ahead of us. We can continue production as planned. The degradation issue would only affect a small percentage of users, and we could address it with a robust warranty program. This would allow us to capitalize on our first-mover advantage and potentially corner the market.

He paused, letting the implications sink in. Several board members nodded, clearly in favor of this option.

"Alternatively," Michael continued, "we can delay the launch by six months to redesign the panel enclosure. This would solve the degradation problem, but it would also mean higher production costs and a later launch. We risk losing our competitive edge."

The silence stretched, heavy with the weight of the decision before them. Michael's mind raced, remembering the words of his grandfather, a small businessman who had weathered many storms: "Plans fail for lack of advice, but with many advisors, they succeed."

As the board erupted into heated discussion, Michael settled back in his chair. He had presented the facts. Now, it was time to listen.

THE ESSENCE OF WISE LEADERSHIP

In the complex landscape of modern business, leadership extends far beyond mere management or decision-making. Wise leadership embraces a broader vision that considers not only immediate profits but also long-term sustainability, ethical implications, and the well-being of all stakeholders.

The ancient proverb, "Where there is no vision, the people perish" (Proverbs 29:18), rings as true in today's boardrooms as it did thousands of years ago. Leaders must provide a clear, ethical vision that inspires and guides their organizations through challenges and opportunities.

Wise leadership in the business context manifests itself in several key ways:

1. **Ethical decision-making**: Putting what's right ahead of what's expedient or immediately profitable.
2. **Long-term vision**: Looking beyond quarterly reports to consider the long-term impact of decisions.
3. **Stakeholder Consideration**: Balancing the needs and interests of all stakeholders, not just shareholders.
4. **Embracing Diverse Perspectives**: Actively seeking out and valuing diverse viewpoints in the decision-making process.

5. **Continue to learn**: Remain humble and open to new ideas and approaches.
6. **Accountability**: Taking responsibility for decisions and their results.
7. **Empowerment**: Fostering leadership in others throughout the organization.

As another proverb wisely counsels, "The fear of the Lord is the beginning of wisdom, and knowledge of the Holy One is understanding" (Proverbs 9:10). In a business context, this can be interpreted as a deep respect for ethical principles and a recognition of one's responsibility to a higher purpose beyond mere profit.

THE BUSINESS CASE FOR WISE LEADERSHIP

While the moral imperative for wise, ethical leadership is clear, it's equally important to recognize its tangible business benefits. Companies led by wise, ethical leaders often outperform their peers over the long term.

1. Trust and Reputation

Wise leaders build trust with all stakeholders-employees, customers, suppliers, and communities. This trust leads to stronger relationships, customer loyalty, and a more resilient business.

Consider the case of Patagonia under the leadership of Yvon Chouinard. By consistently prioritizing environmental sustainability and ethical practices, Patagonia has built a fiercely loyal customer base and a brand value far beyond its size. As the proverb states, "A good name is more desirable than great riches; to be esteemed is better than silver or gold" (Proverbs 22:1).

2. Employee Engagement and Retention

Companies led by wise, ethical leaders attract and retain top talent more effectively. Employees who trust their leaders and believe in their company's mission exhibit higher levels of engagement, productivity, and innovation.

Satya Nadella's leadership at Microsoft exemplifies this principle. By fostering a culture of empathy and continuous learning, Nadella has transformed Microsoft's culture, leading to increased innovation and a tripling of the company's stock price.

3. Resilience and Adaptability

By taking the long view and considering diverse points of view, wise leaders are better equipped to navigate uncertainty and adapt to changing circumstances.

Ed Stack's leadership of Dick's Sporting Goods during the gun control debate demonstrates this resilience. Despite short-term financial hits, Stack's decision to stop selling assault-style weapons and raise the gun-buying age to 21 was consistent with the company's values and ultimately strengthened its brand.

4. Innovation and Growth

By fostering an environment of trust, empowerment,

and ethical behavior, wise leaders create conditions ripe for innovation and sustainable growth

Paul Polman's tenure as CEO of Unilever illustrates this approach. Under his leadership, Unilever committed to ambitious sustainability goals while delivering consistent growth, proving that ethical leadership and profitability can go hand in hand.

5. Risk Management

Wise leaders, with their ethical approach and consideration of long-term consequences, often help their companies avoid the pitfalls of shortsighted or unethical decisions.

James Burke's handling of the 1982 Tylenol crisis at Johnson & Johnson remains a classic example. By putting customer safety ahead of short-term profits, Burke not only managed the immediate crisis, but also enhanced J&J's long-term reputation.

CHALLENGES TO WISE LEADERSHIP

Despite its clear benefits, practicing wise leadership in the modern business environment comes with significant challenges:

1. **Short-Term Pressures**: The demand for quarterly results and constant growth can tempt leaders to prioritize short-term gains over long-term sustainability.

2. **Complexity and Uncertainty**: In a rapidly changing business landscape, leaders must make decisions with incomplete information and unpredictable outcomes.

3. **Stakeholder Balancing**: Different stakeholders often have competing interests, requiring leaders to make difficult trade-offs.

4. **Information Overload**: The sheer volume of data available can paradoxically make decision-making more challenging.

5. **Ethical Dilemmas**: Leaders often face situations where different ethical principles conflict, requiring careful consideration.

6. **Resistance to Change**: Implementing ethical practices or long-term strategies may face resistance from those accustomed to 'business as usual'.

As the proverb warns, "Do not be wise in your own eyes; fear the Lord and shun evil" (Proverbs 3:7). Wise leaders must remain humble, recognizing the complexity of their role and the potential for unintended consequences in their decisions.

STRATEGIES FOR CULTIVATING WISE LEADERSHIP

Developing wise leadership within an organization requires deliberate effort and ongoing commitment. Here are key strategies for fostering wise leadership:

1. Develop a Clear Ethical Framework

Articulate clear ethical principles that guide decision-making throughout the organization. Ensure these principles are communicated effectively and consistently applied.

As the proverb advises, "Let love and faithfulness never leave you; bind them around your neck, write them on the tablet of your heart" (Proverbs 3:3).

2. Foster Diverse Perspectives

Actively seek out and value diverse viewpoints in the decision-making process. Create structures that ensure a variety of voices are heard, from employee resource groups to diverse boards of directors.

3. Implement Ethical Decision-Making Processes

Develop frameworks to help leaders navigate complex ethical decisions. This might include ethics committees, decision trees, or guiding questions to ensure ethical considerations are consistently applied.

4. Invest in Leadership Development

Provide ongoing training and development opportunities focused on ethical leadership, critical thinking, and long-term strategic planning.

5. Practice Transparency

Foster a culture of openness where leaders share the reasoning behind their decisions, admit mistakes, and welcome feedback.

6. Align Incentives with Ethical Behavior

Ensure compensation and promotion structures

reward long-term value creation and ethical behavior rather than short-term results at any cost.

7. Lead by Example

Senior leaders must consistently demonstrate ethical behavior and wise decision-making, especially when it comes at a personal or short-term cost.

8. Encourage Reflection and Learning

Create opportunities for leaders to reflect on their decisions and learn from both successes and failures. As the proverb states, "The wise in heart accept commands, but a chattering fool comes to ruin" (Proverbs 10:8).

THE PATH FORWARD

As the heated discussion in the GreenTech boardroom began to wind down, Michael Rodriguez was at the center of a storm of conflicting opinions. Some board members urged immediate production, arguing that the potential market dominance outweighed the risks. Others urged a delay, citing the long-term reputational damage if the degradation issues became public.

Michael listened intently, weighing each argument. He recalled another piece of wisdom from his grandfather: "The way of fools seems right to them, but the wise listen to advice" (Proverbs 12:15).

As the room fell silent, all eyes turned to Michael. The weight of the decision weighed on him, but he felt a sense of clarity he hadn't expected.

"Thank you all for your insights," he began. "They have been invaluable in considering all aspects of this decision." He paused, meeting the gaze of each board member. "We've always prided ourselves on being at the forefront of sustainable technology. But more than that, we've always prided ourselves on our integrity."

Michael stood, his resolve growing with each word. "We will delay the launch. Yes, it will cost us in the short term. Yes, we risk losing our first-mover advantage. But we can't in good conscience release a product that we know has the potential to fail our customers and harm the environment we're trying to protect.

He held up a hand as murmurs of protest began. "However, we will not simply delay. I'm proposing that we use this time not only to fix the degradation problem but also to explore ways to make the panels more affordable. If we can't be first, let's be the best—in quality, sustainability, and accessibility."

As Michael outlined his vision, he saw the mood in the room change. Skepticism gave way to excitement as board members began to engage with the new direction, offering suggestions and insights.

At that moment, Michael understood the true power of wise leadership. It wasn't about having all the answers or making decisions alone. It was about fostering an environment where ethical considerations were paramount, diverse perspectives were valued, and long-term thinking prevailed.

As leaders navigate the complex landscape of modern business, the wisdom encapsulated in ancient proverbs provides a timeless guide. The challenges may be new, but the principles of wise leadership remain constant:

"Plans fail for lack of counsel, but with many advisers, they succeed." (Proverbs 15:22)

"Where there is no vision, the people perish." (Proverbs 29:18)

"A good name is more desirable than great riches; to be esteemed is better than silver or gold." (Proverbs 22:1)

These proverbs remind us that wise leadership is not about having all the answers but about asking the right questions. It's about valuing diverse perspectives, maintaining a long-term vision, and always striving to do what's right, not just what's expedient.

The path of wise leadership is rarely the easiest. It often requires difficult decisions, short-term sacrifices, and the courage to stand firm in the face of pressure. But as we've seen, it leads not only to lasting success but also to a deeper, more fulfilling experience of business and life.

As we continue our exploration of ancient wisdom in modern business, let these principles of wise leadership guide us. In the chapters to come, we will explore related themes- the value of a good reputation, the importance of fair dealing, and the power of ethical communication. The lessons of wise leadership will serve as a foundation, a constant reminder of the transformative power of ethical decision-making in business.

Let us move forward, guided by the wisdom of the ages, as we continue to explore the rich intersection of ancient principles and modern business practices. In doing so, we can build organizations that are not only financially successful but also positively contribute to our world, creating value far beyond the balance sheet and leaving a lasting, positive legacy.

FIVE

BUILDING A GOOD NAME - THE VALUE OF ETHICAL REPUTATION

"A good name is more desirable than great riches; to be esteemed is better than silver or gold." - Proverbs 22:1

The bustling streets of New York faded to a dull roar as Olivia Hartley stepped into the sleek lobby of Pinnacle Investments. Her heels clicked against the polished marble floor, echoing her racing heartbeat. Today marked a pivotal moment in her career-her first board meeting as the newly appointed Chief Ethics Officer.

Once a darling of Wall Street, Pinnacle was on the brink of a reputational crisis. A series of questionable investment practices had come to light, eroding client confidence and attracting unwelcome scrutiny from regulators. The board had created Olivia's position in a desperate attempt to salvage the firm's tarnished image.

As the elevator climbed to the top floor, Olivia's mind raced through the presentation she'd prepared. She knew her proposals would be met with resistance. In a culture where profit often trumped principle, her call for sweeping ethical reforms would ruffle feathers.

The elevator doors slid open, revealing a panoramic view of the city skyline. Olivia straightened her jacket and strode toward the boardroom, steeling herself for the battle ahead. As she entered, the buzz of conversation died away. A dozen pairs of eyes turned to her, some curious, some skeptical.

"Ms. Hartley," the CEO, Robert Blackwell, greeted her with a thin smile. "We are eager to hear your recommendations for... improving our ethical standing."

Olivia detected a hint of condescension in his tone, but she refused to be intimidated. She sat, opened her laptop, and met Blackwell's gaze.

"Thank you, Mr. Blackwell. Before I begin, I'd like to share a proverb encapsulating the challenge—and the opportunity— before us." She paused, allowing the tension in the room to build. "A good name is more desirable than great riches; to be esteemed is better than silver or gold."

A murmur rippled through the room. Olivia saw a mix of reactions - thoughtful nods, raised eyebrows, barely concealed smirks. She continued, her voice calm and clear.

"Ladies and gentlemen, we are at a crossroads. The path we choose today will determine not only the future of Pinnacle Investments, but also our legacy in the financial world. Will we be remembered as a company that put short-term profits ahead of lasting integrity? Or will we seize this moment to rebuild our reputation and become a beacon of ethical practice in an industry often clouded by distrust?"

As Olivia began her presentation, she knew the road ahead would be challenging. But she also understood a fundamental truth: in the business world, a good name was an asset more valuable than any balance sheet could reflect.

THE ESSENCE OF A GOOD NAME IN BUSINESS

In business, a company's reputation-its "good name-represents much more than just public perception. It embodies the sum total of the organization's actions, values, and impact on the world.. As the proverb wisely counsels, "The name of the righteous is used in blessings, but the name of the wicked will rot" (Proverbs 10:7).

A good name in business manifests in several key ways:

1. **Trust**: The degree to which stakeholders believe in the company's integrity and reliability.
2. **Quality**: Consistently delivering products or services that meet or exceed expectations.
3. **Ethics**: The adherence to moral principles in business practices and decision-making.
4. **Innovation**: The ability to create value through new ideas and approaches.
5. **Social Responsibility**: The company's positive impact on society and the environment.
6. **Transparency**: The willingness to communicate openly and honestly, even in difficult situations.
7. **Customer Focus**: The genuine commitment to meeting customer needs and providing excellent service.

As another proverb reminds us, "A gossip betrays a confidence, but a trustworthy person keeps a secret" (Proverbs 11:13). In the business world, this translates to the importance of maintaining confidentiality, honoring commitments, and being a reliable partner.

THE BUSINESS CASE FOR A GOOD NAME

While the moral imperative for maintaining a good reputation is clear, it's equally important to recognize its tangible business benefits. Companies with strong, positive reputations often outperform their competitors in a variety of ways:

1. Customer Loyalty and Premium Pricing

A good name breeds trust, and trust breeds loyalty. Customers are more likely to stick with brands they trust, and they are often willing to pay a premium for products or services from companies with strong reputations.

Consider the case of Patagonia. The outdoor apparel company's unwavering commitment to environmental sustainability and ethical practices has cultivated a fiercely loyal customer base. Customers are willing to pay premium prices for Patagonia products because they know they support a company that aligns with their values.

2. Talent Attraction and Retention

Companies with strong reputations attract top talent

and retain employees longer. People want to work for organizations they can be proud of and where their work feels meaningful.

Consistently ranked as one of the best places to work, Salesforce exemplifies this principle. The company's strong ethical stance, commitment to equality, and innovative 1-1-1 philanthropy model (donating 1% of product, time, and resources to charity) have made it a magnet for top talent in the competitive technology industry.

3. Crisis Resilience

A good reputation acts as a buffer in times of crisis. Stakeholders are more likely to give companies with strong, positive reputations the benefit of the doubt.

As discussed in earlier chapters, Johnson & Johnson's handling of the 1982 Tylenol crisis demonstrates this principle. The company's swift, transparent response, which put customer safety ahead of short-term profits, managed the immediate crisis and enhanced J&J's long-term reputation.

4. Investor Confidence

Companies with strong ethical reputations often enjoy greater investor confidence, leading to higher valuations and lower costs of capital.

Warren Buffett's Berkshire Hathaway exemplifies this

effect. Buffett's reputation for integrity and long-term value creation has made Berkshire Hathaway shares highly desirable, even at premium prices.

5. Partnerships and Collaborations

A good name opens doors to valuable partnerships and collaborations. Other companies and organizations are more likely to want to work with reputable companies.

Microsoft's transformation under Satya Nadella's leadership is an example of this benefit. By rebuilding Microsoft's reputation as an innovative, collaborative company, Nadella has fostered partnerships with former rivals to expand Microsoft's reach and capabilities.

6. Regulatory Goodwill

Companies known for ethical practices often enjoy better relationships with regulators, which can lead to more favorable treatment when issues arise.

Unilever's proactive stance on sustainability under Paul Polman's leadership has earned the company goodwill with regulators and NGOs. It has helped shape policy discussions and avoided adversarial relationships with regulators

As the proverb states, "The integrity of the upright guides them, but the unfaithful are destroyed by their duplicity" (Proverbs 11:3). In the long run, companies that prioritize their reputation find that it leads to sustainable success, while those that neglect their reputation for short-term gains often face dire consequences.

CHALLENGES TO BUILDING AND MAINTAINING A GOOD NAME

Despite the clear benefits, building and maintaining a good reputation in today's business environment presents significant challenges:

1. **Short-Term Pressures**: The demand for quick profits can lead companies to make decisions that improve short-term results at the expense of long-term reputation.
2. **Transparency in the Digital Age:** With social media and instant global communication, companies operate under constant scrutiny. A single misstep can quickly escalate into a reputational crisis.
3. **Complex Supply Chains**: As supply chains span the globe, ensuring ethical practices throughout becomes increasingly challenging.
4. **Diverse Stakeholder Expectations**: Different stakeholders may have conflicting expectations, making it difficult to satisfy everyone while maintaining a consistent ethical stance.
5. **Industry Norms**: In industries where unethical practices have become normalized, taking an ethical stance can put a company at a short-term competitive disadvantage.
6. **Rapid Technological Change**: Emerging technologies often present new ethical challenges before societal norms and regulations have caught up.

7. **Cultural Differences**: Global companies must navigate diverse cultural norms and expectations while maintaining a consistent ethical core.

As the proverb warns, "Like a muddied spring or a polluted well are the righteous who give way to the wicked" (Proverbs 25:26). Companies must remain vigilant against compromising their values, even when faced with significant pressures or temptations.

STRATEGIES FOR BUILDING AND MAINTAINING A GOOD NAME

Cultivating a positive reputation requires deliberate effort and ongoing commitment. Here are key strategies for building and maintaining a good name in business:

1. Define and Communicate Clear Values

Articulate a clear set of values that guide all aspects of the organization. Ensure that these values are effectively communicated to all stakeholders and consistently applied in decision-making.

As the proverb advises, "Above all else, guard your heart, for everything you do flows from it" (Proverbs 4:23). In a business context, this speaks to the importance of maintaining a strong ethical core.

2. Lead by Example

Leaders must embody the company's values in their actions and decisions. As another proverb states, "Like a coating of silver dross on earthenware are fervent lips with an evil heart" (Proverbs 26:23). Actions speak louder than words, and ethical leadership sets the tone for the entire organization.

3. Foster a Culture of Integrity

Create an environment in which ethical behavior is expected and rewarded. Implement systems to encourage and protect whistleblowers, and ensure that ethical considerations are part of every major decision.

4. Prioritize Transparency

Be open and honest in communications, even when it's difficult. Address issues proactively rather than waiting for them to become crises.

5. Invest in Quality and Innovation

Consistently deliver high-quality products or services. Invest in innovation to create genuine value for customers and society.

6. Engage in Meaningful Corporate Social Responsibility

Develop CSR initiatives that align with the company's values and core competencies. Avoid "greenwashing" or superficial philanthropy.

7. Cultivate Strong Stakeholder Relationships

Build and maintain positive relationships with all

stakeholders, including customers, employees, investors, suppliers, communities, and even regulators.

8. Implement Robust Ethics Training

Conduct ongoing ethics training for all employees, focusing on practical application in daily decision-making.

9. Monitor and Manage Your Reputation

Assess your company's reputation with various stakeholder groups regularly. Develop and maintain a crisis management plan to address potential reputational threats.

10. Learn from Mistakes

When errors occur, openly acknowledge them, take corrective action, and implement changes to prevent recurrence. As the proverb suggests, "Whoever conceals their sins does not prosper, but the one who confesses and renounces them finds mercy" (Proverbs 28:13).

THE PATH FORWARD

As Olivia Hartley finished her presentation, a heavy silence fell over the Pinnacle Investments boardroom. She had laid out a comprehensive plan for ethical reform-from revamping investment practices to implementing rigorous ethics training, from increasing transparency to engaging in meaningful corporate social responsibility.

The CEO, Robert Blackwell, leaned forward, his brow furrowed. "Ms. Hartley, your proposals are... ambitious. But in this industry, we operate in shades of gray. Can we really afford to be so... uncompromising?"

Olivia met his gaze. "Mr. Blackwell, fellow board members, I submit that we cannot afford not to. Yes, the path I'm proposing is challenging. Yes, it may affect our short-term profits. But consider the alternative."

She gestured to a slide showing Pinnacle's plummeting stock price and customer exodus. "Our current trajectory is unsustainable. We're hemorrhaging customers, our stock is in free fall, and regulators are circling. But more than that, we're losing something even more precious-our good name.

Olivia's voice grew passionate. "A wise proverb tells us, 'The hatred of the righteous is lying lips, but the righteous love the one who speaks truth' (Proverbs 13:5). Our clients, our employees, our communities—they're yearning for a financial institution they can trust. By committing to unwavering ethical practices, we have the opportunity to become that institution."

She paused, letting her words sink in. "Yes, this path is difficult. Yes, it requires courage. But I believe it's not only the right thing to do-it's our best path to long-term success and sustainability.

As the discussion raged around the table, Olivia saw a glimmer of something in Blackwell's eyes-was it recognition? Hope? She couldn't be sure, but she knew she had opened the door to a new possibility for Pinnacle.

Similar conversations are taking place in boardrooms and offices around the world. As companies grapple with ethical challenges and reputational crises, the wisdom encapsulated in ancient proverbs provides a timeless guide. The challenges may be new, but the principles of building and maintaining a good name remain constant:

> *"A good name is more desirable than great riches; to be esteemed is better than silver or gold." (Proverbs 22:1)*

> *"The name of the righteous is used in blessings, but the name of the wicked will rot." (Proverbs 10:7)*

> *"The integrity of the upright guides them, but the unfaithful are destroyed by their duplicity." (Proverbs 11:3)*

These proverbs remind us that a good name is not just a nice-to-have asset, but a fundamental driver of long-term business success. It's the basis for trust, the catalyst for loyalty, and the foundation for sustainable growth.

The path to building and maintaining a good reputation is rarely easy. It requires constant vigilance, the courage to make tough decisions, and a commitment to putting principle before short-term gain. But as we've seen, it's a path that leads not only to lasting success but also to a deeper, more fulfilling way of doing business.

As we continue our exploration of ancient wisdom in modern business, let these principles of ethical reputation guide us. In the chapters that follow, we will explore related themes-the importance of integrity in leadership, the power of ethical communication, and the role of business in creating positive social impact. Throughout, the lessons learned about the value of a good name will serve as a foundation, a constant reminder of the transformative power of ethical business practices.

Let us move forward, guided by the wisdom of the ages, as we continue to explore the rich intersection of ancient principles and modern business practices. In doing so, we can build organizations that are not only financially successful but also make a positive contribution to our world, creating value far beyond the balance sheet and leaving a lasting, positive legacy.

SIX
ETHICAL EMPLOYEE RELATIONS - TREATING WORKERS JUSTLY

"Those who oppress the poor to increase their wealth and those who give gifts to the rich—both come to poverty." - Proverbs 22:16

The factory floor buzzed with activity as conveyor belts whirred and workers moved with practiced efficiency. Amanda Chen, the newly appointed CEO of Global Textiles Inc., walked the production line, her keen eyes taking in every detail. The company had built its success on fast fashion, churning out trendy clothes at breakneck speed to satisfy consumers' insatiable appetite.

But at what cost?

As Amanda watched the workers- their tired eyes, their repetitive motions, the grim conditions of the factory-a feeling of unease settled in her stomach. She'd determinedly climbed the corporate ladder, always focused on the bottom line. Standing among the people who made that bottom line possible, she questioned everything.

A young worker caught her eye - a girl who couldn't have been more than eighteen, her fingers moving at lightning speed as she sewed seams. Amanda approached her with a warm smile. "Hi, I'm Amanda Chen, the new CEO. What's your name?"

The girl looked up, startled. Fear flashed across her face before she collected herself. "Lin, ma'am. Lin Wei."

"How long have you worked here, Lin?"

"Three years, ma'am."

Amanda did the math quickly. Fifteen when she started. She probably supports her family. Working long hours in conditions Amanda would never accept for herself.

As she continued her tour, Amanda's mind raced. The board had brought her in to increase profits and streamline operations. But standing here, faced with the human cost of those profits, she faced a moral dilemma she couldn't ignore.

Back in her office, Amanda sank into her chair, the weight of her observations pressing down on her. She pulled out a small, worn book—a collection of proverbs her grandmother had given her years ago. Her eyes fell on a passage: "Those who oppress the poor to increase their wealth and those who give gifts to the rich—both come to poverty."

The words hit her like a punch in the gut. Was this what she had been doing her entire career? Oppressing the poor in order to increase wealth? As she considered the way forward, Amanda knew one thing for sure: things were about to change at Global Textiles.

THE ESSENCE OF ETHICAL EMPLOYEE RELATIONS

In the complex ecosystem of modern business, people are far more than resources or assets on a balance sheet. They are the lifeblood of any organization, the driving force behind innovation, productivity and, ultimately, success. Ethical employee relations go beyond compliance with labor laws; they embody a fundamental respect for human dignity and a commitment to fairness, growth and mutual prosperity.

As another proverb wisely counsels, "A worker's appetite works for him; his hunger drives him on" (Proverbs 16:26). This speaks to the intrinsic motivation of employees when they are treated fairly and their basic needs are met. Ethical employee relations harness this natural drive, creating an environment where employees can thrive and, in turn, drive the organization forward.

Key aspects of ethical employee relations include:

1. **Fair Compensation**: Provide wages and benefits that enable employees to meet their basic needs and support their families.
2. **Safe Working Conditions**: Ensure a work environment free from unnecessary hazards and risks to physical and mental health.
3. **Work-Life Balance**: Respect employees' time outside of work and promote a healthy work-life balance.
4. **Professional Development**: Provide opportunities for skill enhancement, career growth, and personal development.
5. **Inclusivity and Diversity**: Foster a workplace where all individuals, regardless of background or identity, are respected and valued.

6. **Open Communication**: Maintain transparent channels for dialogue between management and employees.
7. **Employee Empowerment**: Give employees a voice in decisions that affect their work and the organization as a whole.
8. **Recognition and Appreciation**: Recognize and reward employee contributions and achievements.

As the proverb states, "One who oppresses the poor to increase his wealth and one who gives gifts to the rich—both come to poverty" (Proverbs 22:16). This serves as a stark reminder of the long-term consequences of exploitative labor practices and the importance of equitable treatment across all levels of an organization.

THE BUSINESS CASE FOR ETHICAL EMPLOYEE RELATIONS

While the moral imperative to treat workers fairly is clear, it's equally important to recognize the tangible business benefits of ethical employee relations. Companies that prioritize fair and respectful treatment of their employees often outperform their competitors in a variety of ways:

1. Increased Productivity and Innovation

When employees are treated fairly and feel valued, they are more likely to go above and beyond in their work. They bring more energy, creativity, and commitment to their roles.

Consider the case of Costco. The retail giant is known for offering the highest wages and benefits in the retail industry. As a result, Costco enjoys significantly higher productivity per employee than its competitors, along with lower turnover rates and higher customer satisfaction.

2. Enhanced Employee Retention and Reduced Turnover Costs

Treating employees ethically builds loyalty. Companies with strong ethical practices often have lower turnover rates, which reduces the cost of hiring and training new employees.

Patagonia, the outdoor clothing company, exemplifies this principle. Its commitment to work-life balance, environmental values, and employee well-being has resulted in a turnover rate far below the industry average, saving millions in employee retention costs each year.

3. Improved Company Reputation and Brand Value

A company's treatment of its employees doesn't stop at the office door. In the age of social media and glass-door.com reviews, a reputation for ethical employee relations can significantly enhance a company's brand equity and customer appeal.

Microsoft's transformation under Satya Nadella's leadership illustrates this effect. By fostering a more inclusive and empowering culture, Microsoft has become a more attractive employer and seen its brand value and stock price soar.

4. Increased Resilience and Adaptability

Companies with strong, positive relationships with their employees are better equipped to navigate challenges and adapt to changing circumstances. Employees who feel respected and valued are likelier to support the company through difficult times and embrace necessary changes.

Toyota's response to the 2008 financial crisis illustrates this principle. Instead of laying off workers, the company used the downturn as an opportunity for training and process improvement. This approach maintained morale and positioned Toyota for a strong recovery when market conditions improved.

5. Attraction of Top Talent

In a competitive job market, a reputation for treating employees ethically can be a key differentiator in attracting top talent.

Google's early reputation as a great place to work, with its innovative perks and focus on employee well-being, allowed the company to attract some of the brightest minds in technology, fueling its rapid growth and innovation.

6. Enhanced Customer Service

Employees who are treated well are more likely to treat customers well. This translates into better customer service, increased customer loyalty, and ultimately, better business results.

The Four Seasons hotel chain is known for its exceptional customer service, which is directly linked to its treatment of employees. By investing heavily in employee training, empowerment and well-being, Four Seasons has created a workforce that consistently delivers world-class service to guests.

As the proverb reminds us, "The righteous care about justice for the poor, but the wicked have no such concern" (Proverbs 29:7). In the long run, companies that prioritize fair treatment of their workers find that it leads to sustainable success, while those that exploit their workers for short-term gain often face dire consequences.

CHALLENGES TO ETHICAL EMPLOYEE RELATIONS

Despite the clear benefits, maintaining ethical employee relations in the modern business environment presents significant challenges:

1. **Short-Term Financial Pressures**: The demand for quick profits can lead companies to cut corners on employee benefits or working conditions.
2. **Global Competition**: Companies may feel pressure to reduce labor costs to compete with companies operating in countries with lower wage standards or less stringent labor laws.
3. **Rapid Technological Change**: Automation and AI are reshaping the nature of work, creating uncertainty and potential job displacement.

4. **Diverse Workforce Needs**: With multiple generations and cultures in the workplace, meeting the diverse needs and expectations of all employees can be complex.

5. **Gig Economy and Non-Traditional Employment**: The rise of contract and temporary work poses new challenges to ensuring fair treatment and benefits.

6. **Work-Life Balance in a Connected World**: Technology has blurred the lines between work and personal time, making it difficult to ensure that employees can truly disconnect.

7. **Mental Health and Workplace Stress**: Increasing awareness of mental health issues requires companies to address not only the physical, but also the mental well-being of their employees.

As the proverb warns, "Do not exploit the poor because they are poor and do not crush the needy in court, for the Lord will take up their case and will exact life for life" (Proverbs 22:22-23). Companies must remain vigilant against the temptation to exploit vulnerable workers, even when faced with significant economic pressures.

STRATEGIES FOR FOSTERING ETHICAL EMPLOYEE RELATIONS

Establishing and maintaining ethical employee relations requires conscious effort and ongoing commitment. Here are key strategies for promoting fair treatment of workers:

1. Develop and Communicate Clear Ethical Standards

Articulate a clear set of ethical principles for employee relations. Ensure that these standards are effectively communicated to all levels of the organization and consistently applied in decision-making.

As the proverb advises, "The tongue of the righteous is choice silver, but the heart of the wicked is of little value" (Proverbs 10:20). Clear, ethical communication sets the tone for the entire organization.

2. Ensure Fair Compensation and Benefits

Review and adjust compensation packages regularly to ensure they meet or exceed living wage standards. Consider innovative benefits that meet employees' diverse needs.

3. Invest in Employee Development

Create robust training and development programs that enable employees to grow their skills and advance their careers within the organization.

4. Foster Work-Life Balance

Implement policies that respect employees' time away from work, such as flexible work schedules, remote work options, and generous paid time off.

5. Prioritize Workplace Safety and Well-being

Go beyond minimum safety standards to create a work environment that actively promotes both physical and mental well-being.

6. Promote Diversity and Inclusion

Develop programs and policies that foster a diverse workforce and an inclusive culture where all employees feel valued and respected.

7. Empower Employee Voice

Create channels for employees to provide feedback, raise concerns, and contribute ideas without fear of retaliation. Consider implementing employee representation in decision-making processes.

8. Lead by Example

Leaders must embody the company's ethical standards in their actions and decisions. As another proverb states, "Like a coating of silver dross on earthenware are fervent lips with an evil heart" (Proverbs 26:23). Actions speak louder than words.

9. Regular Ethical Audits

Conduct regular assessments of your employee relations practices, seeking input from employees at all levels of the organization.

10. Extend Ethical Practices to Supply Chain

Ensure that ethical employee relations extend beyond your immediate workforce to include suppliers and contractors.

THE PATH FORWARD

As the sun dipped below the horizon, casting long shadows across her office, Amanda Chen sat deep in thought. Observations from her factory tour and the wisdom of proverbs swirled in her mind, coalescing into a vision of what Global Textiles should become.

She began to formulate a plan. First, a comprehensive audit of working conditions and compensation at all its facilities. Then, a phased approach to improvements: better safety measures, fair wage adjustments, reduced working hours, and investments in employee training and development.

Amanda knew the board would balk at the costs. But she also knew she had to try. She recalled another proverb: "Speak up for those who cannot speak for themselves, for the rights of all who are destitute. Speak up and judge fairly; defend the rights of the poor and needy" (Proverbs 31:8-9).

With renewed determination, she began drafting her proposal. It wouldn't be easy, but she was convinced it was not only the right thing to do, but also the key to the long-term success and sustainability of Global Textiles.

Weeks later, Amanda stood before the board of directors, her heart racing but her voice steady. "Ladies and gentlemen, I stand before you today not only as your CEO but as someone who has seen firsthand the human cost of our current practices. We have built our success on the backs of workers who can barely make ends meet, who work in conditions we wouldn't accept for ourselves or our children."

She paused, letting her words sink in. "But I'm not here to dwell on the mistakes of the past. I'm here to propose a new way forward that aligns with our values, enhances our reputation, and ultimately improves our bottom line."

As Amanda outlined her plan for ethical employee relations, she saw a mix of reactions around the table. Skepticism, concern, but also glimmers of interest and hope.

"I know what you're thinking," she went on. "This will be expensive. It will eat into our profits, at least in the short term. But consider this: our current model is unsustainable. We face increasing consumer scrutiny, potential regulation, and the very real risk of losing our workforce to competitors who treat them better."

She clicked on a slide showing projections of increased productivity, reduced turnover, and enhanced brand equity. "By investing in our people, we are investing in our future. We create a workforce that is more productive, innovative, and loyal. We are building a brand that customers can trust, and that employees are proud to work for.

As the discussion raged around the table, Amanda knew she had opened the door to a new opportunity for Global Textiles. The road ahead would be challenging, but she was determined to see it through.

Similar conversations are taking place in boardrooms and offices around the world. As companies grapple with the complexities of modern employment and the ethical implications of their labor practices, the wisdom encapsulated in ancient proverbs provides a timeless guide. The challenges may be new, but the principles of treating workers fairly remain constant:

"Those who oppress the poor to increase their wealth and those who give gifts to the rich—both come to poverty." (Proverbs 22:16)

"The righteous care about justice for the poor, but the wicked have no such concern." (Proverbs 29:7)

"Speak up for those who cannot speak for themselves, for the rights of all who are destitute. Speak up and judge fairly; defend the rights of the poor and needy." (Proverbs 31:8-9)

These proverbs remind us that ethical employee relations are not just a legal or public relations issue but a fundamental driver of long-term business success. They are the foundation of an engaged workforce, a positive corporate culture, and a sustainable business model.

The road to ethical employee relations is rarely easy. It requires constant vigilance, the courage to make difficult decisions, and a commitment to putting people before short-term profits. But as we've seen, it's a path that leads to sustainable success and a deeper, more fulfilling way of doing business.

As we continue our exploration of ancient wisdom in modern business, let these principles of just treatment of workers guide us. In the chapters to come, we will explore related themes, such as the importance of ethical leadership, the power of corporate social responsibility, and the role of business in creating positive social impact. The lessons learned about ethical employee relations will serve as a foundation, a constant reminder of the transformative power of treating workers with dignity and respect.

Let us move forward, guided by the wisdom of the ages, as we continue to explore the rich intersection of ancient principles and modern business practices. In doing so, we can build organizations that succeed financially and positively contribute to the lives of their employees and society at large - creating value far beyond the balance sheet and leaving a lasting, positive legacy.

SEVEN

THE WISDOM OF LONG-TERM THINKING

"*Dishonest money dwindles away, but whoever gathers money little by little makes it grow.*" - *Proverbs 13:11*

The gleaming skyscraper of FutureTech Innovations pierced the San Francisco skyline, its glass and steel facade reflecting the golden hues of the setting sun. On the 50th floor, CEO Daniel Hawthorne stood before a wall of windows, his gaze fixed on the bustling city below. His reflection stared back at him, the lines on his face etched deeper than usual, his eyes clouded with worry.

FutureTech, once the darling of Silicon Valley, was now teetering on the brink of crisis. Its revolutionary AI-powered personal assistant, touted as the next big leap in consumer technology, had hit a major snag. Early adopters reported alarming privacy breaches, with the AI accessing and sharing sensitive information without user consent.

The PR nightmare had sent the company's stock plummeting, and now, just hours before a crucial board meeting, Daniel was grappling with the most difficult decision of his career.

A gentle knock on the door interrupted his thoughts. "Come in," he called, not turning from the window.

Sarah Chen, FutureTech's Chief Technology Officer, entered, her typically confident stride subdued. "Daniel, I have the latest report on the AI's core algorithm. It's... not good."

Daniel turned and met Sarah's worried gaze. "Give it to me straight."

Sarah took a deep breath. "The privacy issues are more deeply rooted than we first thought. Fixing them would require a complete overhaul of the AI's learning patterns. We're looking at at least six months, possibly a year, before we could relaunch."

Daniel clenched his jaw. One year. In the fast-paced world of technology, a year could be an eternity. He could already hear the board's objections and the shareholders' outrage.

"What about a patch?" he asked, knowing the answer before the words left his mouth.

Sarah shook her head. "A patch would be a Band-Aid on a gunshot wound. It might stop the bleeding temporarily, but it won't solve the underlying problem. Worse, it might give our users a false sense of security."

Daniel nodded and turned back to the window. The city lights began to flicker, a constellation of human activity unfolding before him. Each light represented a potential user, a person whose trust they'd betrayed, whose privacy they'd compromised.

His grandfather's voice echoed in his mind, a memory from his childhood visits to the old man's small electronics repair shop. "Remember, Danny," he'd say, his weathered hands carefully reassembling a circuit board, "Dishonest money dwindles away, but whoever gathers money little by little makes it grow."

At the time, Daniel had nodded politely, more interested in the shiny new gadgets on the store shelves than in his grandfather's old-fashioned wisdom. Now, those words carried a weight he'd never fully appreciated.

"Sarah," he said, his decision crystallizing, "prepare a full report on the overhaul process. Timeline, resource requirements, everything. We will do this right, no matter how long it takes."

Sarah's eyes widened. "The board won't like it. The shareholders will revolt."

"Probably," Daniel agreed, a wry smile tugging at his lips. "But I'd rather face their wrath now than destroy the trust of our users forever. We built this company on the promise of improving people's lives. It's time we lived up to that promise, even if it hurts in the short term."

As Sarah left to prepare the report, Daniel returned to the cityscape, the weight of his decision settling on his shoulders. The path ahead would be difficult, but he knew in his heart it was the right one. In a world obsessed with quick profits and instant gratification, the wisdom of long-term thinking might be their only salvation.

THE ESSENCE OF LONG-TERM THINKING IN BUSINESS

In today's fast-paced, ever-changing business environment, the pressure to deliver immediate results often overshadows the importance of long-term planning and sustainable growth. Yet, as the ancient proverb reminds us, "The plans of the diligent lead to profit as surely as haste leads to poverty" (Proverbs 21:5).

Long-term thinking in business encompasses several key principles:

1. **Sustainable Growth**: Prioritize steady, consistent growth over rapid, unsustainable expansion.
2. **Investment in Innovation**: Allocate resources to research and development, even if the payoff isn't immediate.
3. **Stakeholder Value**: Consider the long-term interests of all stakeholders, not just short-term shareholder returns.
4. **Environmental Stewardship**: Implement practices that ensure the long-term health of the environment and the communities in which we operate.
5. **Talent Development**: Invest in employee growth and development, to build a skilled and loyal workforce over time.
6. **Brand Building**: Focus on creating lasting brand value rather than short-term revenue spikes.
7. **Financial Prudence**: Maintain a strong balance sheet and avoid excessive debt to weather economic downturns.

As another proverb wisely states, "The wise store up choice food and olive oil, but fools gulp theirs down" (Proverbs 21:20). In business terms, this speaks to the importance of reinvesting profits, building reserves, and preparing for future challenges and opportunities.

THE BUSINESS CASE FOR LONG-TERM THINKING

While the pressure for quick wins and quarterly results can be intense, companies that think long-term often outperform their myopic counterparts in a variety of ways:

1. Sustained Competitive Advantage

Companies that invest in long-term strategies often develop unique capabilities and resources that are difficult for competitors to quickly replicate.

Consider the case of Amazon. For years, the company has prioritized growth and reinvestment over short-term profits, building an unparalleled e-commerce infrastructure and expanding into new markets. This long-term approach has resulted in a dominant market position and substantial profits in recent years.

2. Innovation Leadership

Long-term thinking allows companies to invest in ambitious, potentially game-changing innovations that may not yield immediate returns.

Apple's development of the iPhone is an example of this approach. The company invested heavily in research and development and redefined the mobile phone market. While the initial investment was substantial, the long-term payoff has been enormous, making Apple one of the most valuable companies in the world.

3. Brand Loyalty and Trust

Companies that prioritize long-term customer relationships over short-term sales often build stronger brand loyalty and customer trust.

Outdoor clothing company Patagonia has built its brand on a long-term commitment to environmental sustainability and product quality. This approach has cultivated a fiercely loyal customer base willing to pay premium prices for its products.

4. Resilience in Economic Downturns

Companies with a long-term focus often build stronger balance sheets and more diversified revenue streams, enabling them to weather economic storms more effectively.

During the 2008 financial crisis, companies like Johnson & Johnson, with their strong balance sheet and diversified product portfolio, were able to weather the downturn better than many of their peers.

5. Attracting Long-Term Investors

A focus on long-term value creation attracts investors

who are aligned with the company's vision and less likely to push for short-term results at the expense of long-term health.

Under Warren Buffett's leadership, Berkshire Hathaway has consistently attracted investors who appreciate its long-term, value-oriented approach. This stable investor base has allowed the company to make decisions focused on long-term value creation.

6. Talent Retention and Development

Companies that are known for taking the long view often attract and retain top talent more effectively because employees see opportunities for growth and development.

Google's approach to talent management, which includes significant investments in employee development and innovative perks, has helped the company become one of the most sought-after employers in the technology industry.

As the proverb states, "The simple inherit folly, but the prudent are crowned with knowledge" (Proverbs 14:18). In the business world, this wisdom underscores the long-term benefits of thoughtful, strategic decision-making over short-sighted actions.

CHALLENGES TO LONG-TERM THINKING

Despite its clear benefits, maintaining a long-term focus in today's business environment presents significant challenges:

1. **Quarterly Earnings Pressure**: Public companies face intense pressure to meet or exceed quarterly earnings expectations, which can lead to short-term decision-making at the expense of long-term value creation.

2. **Short-Term Incentive Structures**: Many executive compensation packages are tied to short-term performance metrics, which can misalign management's interests with the long-term health of the company.

3. **Rapid Technological Change**: In fast-moving industries, the fear of being left behind can drive companies to make hasty decisions rather than thoughtful, long-term plans.

4. **Market Volatility**: Fluctuations in stock prices and market sentiment can create pressure for quick fixes rather than sustainable strategies.

5. **Shareholder Activism**: Some activist investors push for immediate returns through cost cutting, divestitures, or other short-term measures, potentially at the expense of long-term growth.

6. **Competitive Pressures**: In highly competitive markets, companies may feel compelled to prioritize short-term market share gains over long-term sustainable growth.

As the proverb warns, "One who is quick-tempered acts foolishly, and one who devises evil schemes is hated" (Proverbs 14:17). In business, this can be interpreted as a caution against reactive, short-term decisions and unethical practices aimed at quick gains.

STRATEGIES FOR CULTIVATING LONG-TERM THINKING

Fostering a culture of long-term thinking requires deliberate effort and ongoing commitment. Here are key strategies for fostering a long-term mindset in your organization:

1. **Articulate a Clear Long-Term Vision**: Develop and communicate a compelling long-term vision for the organization. Ensure that all stakeholders understand and buy into the vision.

    As the proverb advises, "Where there is no vision, the people perish" (Proverbs 29:18). A clear, inspiring long-term vision provides direction and motivation for the entire organization.

2. **Align Incentives with Long-Term Goals**: Redesign compensation and performance evaluation systems to reward long-term value creation rather than short-term results.

3. **Invest in Sustainable Practices**: Implement environmentally and socially responsible practices that ensure the long-term sustainability of the business and its ecosystem.

4. **Foster a Culture of Innovation**: Create an environment that encourages experimentation and learning, even if it means accepting short-term setbacks for long-term gains.

5. **Build Strong Stakeholder Relationships**: Prioritize building lasting relationships with customers, employees, suppliers, and communities, recognizing that these relationships are key to long-term success.

6. **Practice Financial Discipline**: Maintain a strong balance sheet and avoid excessive debt, ensuring the company has the financial flexibility to weather downturns and invest in long-term opportunities.

7. **Communicate Long-Term Metrics**: Develop and report on key performance indicators that reflect long-term value creation, not just short-term financial results.

8. **Invest in Employee Development**: Create robust training and development programs that help employees improve their skills and advance their careers within the organization.

9. **Embrace Scenario Planning**: Conduct regular scenario planning exercises to anticipate and prepare for potential long-term changes in the business environment.

10. **Lead by Example**: Leaders must consistently demonstrate commitment to long-term thinking in their decisions and actions, setting the tone for the entire organization.

As the proverb states, "The path of the righteous is like the morning sun, shining ever brighter till the full light of day" (Proverbs 4:18). This wisdom encapsulates the gradual but powerful impact of consistent, long-term thinking in business.

THE PATH FORWARD

As the board meeting approached, Daniel Hawthorne stood before his executive team, the weight of FutureTech's future on his shoulders. He'd spent the night poring over Sarah's report, mapping out scenarios and steeling himself for the battle ahead.

"Ladies and gentlemen," he began, his voice steady and determined, "we stand at a crossroads. The path of least resistance beckons - a quick patch, a PR campaign, a return to business as usual. It's the path many would expect us to take."

He paused, meeting every pair of eyes around the table. "But that's not the way we want to go."

Murmurs of surprise rippled through the room. Daniel held up a hand to silence them.

"We built this company on a promise - to make technology that actually improves people's lives. We've strayed from that promise, and now we have a choice. We can continue down this path of putting short-term profits before the trust of our users, or we can take the harder road. We can admit our mistakes, return to the drawing board, and create something worthy of the FutureTech name."

He clicked a button and Sarah's report appeared on the screen behind him. "This is our roadmap for the next year. A complete overhaul of our AI's core algorithms. New privacy safeguards. Transparent data practices. It won't be easy. Our stock will take a beating. The media will have a field day. But at the end of this road, we'll have a product we can be proud of - one that truly serves our users, not exploits them.

The room fell silent as the implications sank in. Then, slowly, nods of agreement began to spread.

"There's an old proverb my grandfather used to quote," Daniel continued, a small smile playing on his lips. "'The plans of the diligent lead to profit as surely as haste leads to poverty.' We've been hasty, and we've paid the price. Now it's time for diligence. For patience. For thinking beyond the next quarter to the next decade and beyond."

As the meeting adjourned and his team filed out, energized by the new direction, Daniel felt a weight lift from his shoulders. The road ahead would be challenging, but he knew in his heart it was the right one.

Similar decisions are made every day in boardrooms and offices around the world. As companies grapple with the pressures of a fast-paced, ever-changing global economy, the wisdom encapsulated in ancient proverbs provides a timeless guide. The challenges may be new, but the principles of long-term thinking remain constant:

"Dishonest money dwindles away, but whoever gathers money little by little makes it grow." (Proverbs 13:11)

"The plans of the diligent lead to profit as surely as haste leads to poverty." (Proverbs 21:5)

"The path of the righteous is like the morning sun, shining ever brighter till the full light of day." (Proverbs 4:18)

These proverbs remind us that true success in business isn't measured in quarterly reports or daily stock fluctuations. It's built day by day, decision by decision, through a consistent commitment to ethical practices, sustainable growth, and long-term value creation.

The path of long-term thinking is rarely the easiest. It requires courage to resist short-term pressures, wisdom to navigate uncertainty, and patience to see strategies through to fruition. But as we've seen, it's a path that leads not only to sustainable success but also to a deeper, more fulfilling way of doing business.

As we continue our exploration of ancient wisdom in modern business, let these principles of long-term thinking guide us. In the chapters to come, we will explore related themes-the importance of legacy building, the power of patient capital, and the role of business in creating lasting social value. Throughout, the lessons learned about the wisdom of long-term thinking will serve as a foundation, a constant reminder of the transformative power of looking beyond the immediate horizon.

Let us move forward, guided by the wisdom of the ages, as we continue to explore the rich intersection of ancient principles and modern business practices. In doing so, we can build organizations that not only succeed financially but also make a positive contribution to our world - creating value that extends far beyond the balance sheet and leaving a lasting, positive legacy for generations to come.

EIGHT

ETHICAL COMMUNICATION – TRUTH TELLING IN BUSINESS

"*T*he Lord detests lying lips, but he delights in people who are trustworthy." - *Proverbs 12:22*

The sleek conference room at MediCore Pharmaceuticals buzzed with nervous energy. Rachel Thompson, the newly appointed head of communications, stood at the head of the table, her heart pounding beneath her carefully composed exterior. Before she sat with the company's executive team, their faces were a mixture of concern and expectation.

MediCore was facing its biggest crisis in decades. Its flagship pain medication, hailed as a breakthrough in non-addictive pain management, had been linked to serious side effects in a small but significant number of patients. The undisclosed findings threatened to unravel years of research, development, and marketing.

Rachel's predecessor had been quietly let go for trying to bury the report. Now, all eyes were on her, waiting to hear her strategy for navigating these treacherous waters.

"Ladies and gentlemen," Rachel began, her voice steady despite the butterflies in her stomach, "we are at a critical juncture. The easy path lies before us - we could downplay these findings, bury them in scientific jargon, or worse, suppress them altogether."

She paused, meeting every pair of eyes around the table. "But I'm here to tell you why we must reject that path entirely."

A gasp of surprise rippled through the room. Rachel saw the CEO, Dr. James Chen, lean forward, his brow furrowed.

"Ms. Thompson," he interjected, his tone cautious, "while I appreciate your... idealism, you must understand the stakes. This drug represents billions in revenue and years of work. Surely there's a middle ground?"

Rachel took a deep breath, steeling herself. "Dr. Chen, esteemed colleagues, I understand the stakes all too well. But consider this - what happens when the truth inevitably comes out? And it will come out. What will it cost us then, not only in dollars but in trust?"

She clicked a button, and a series of graphs appeared on the screen behind her. "This is what happened to companies that chose to hide or downplay similar problems. In the short term, they saved face. Long-term? Bankruptcy. Criminal charges. Irreparable damage to your reputation."

The room fell silent as the implications sank in. Rachel continued, her voice growing more passionate. "There's an old proverb my grandmother used to quote: 'The Lord detests lying lips, but he delights in people who are trustworthy.' In business terms, our stakeholders - our patients, doctors, investors, and the public - they are looking for trustworthiness. And in this age of rapid information flow, trust is our most valuable asset."

She clicked to the next slide, revealing a comprehensive communications strategy. "I propose full transparency. We get out in front of this story. We announce the findings ourselves, express genuine concern for the patients affected, and detail our plan to address the issue. Yes, our stock will take a hit. Yes, we'll face scrutiny. But we'll weather that storm with our integrity intact, and in the long run, we'll be stronger for it."

As Rachel outlined her plan, she saw a shift in the room. Skepticism gave way to thoughtful consideration. Even Dr. Chen's expression softened, a glimmer of respect in his eyes.

When she finished, Dr. Chen leaned back in his chair, a wry smile playing on his lips. "Ms. Thompson, when we hired you, we were expecting a spin doctor. Instead, it seems we've found a truth-teller. It's a bold strategy. Risky. But... I think it's just what we need."

As the meeting adjourned and the executives filed out, the air filled with lively discussion, Rachel felt a weight lift from her shoulders. The road ahead would be challenging, but she knew in her heart it was the right one. In a world often clouded by corporate doublespeak and evasion, the clarity of truth could be her most powerful ally.

THE ESSENCE OF ETHICAL COMMUNICATION IN BUSINESS

In the complex landscape of modern business, communication is the lifeblood of organizations, flowing between employees, customers, investors, and the public. Ethical communication goes beyond the mere exchange of information; it embodies a commitment to honesty, transparency, and respect for all stakeholders.

As another proverb wisely counsels, "The tongue has the power of life and death, and those who love it will eat its fruit" (Proverbs 18:21). In a business context, this underscores the profound impact our words can have - they can build trust or destroy it, inspire confidence or sow doubt.

Key aspects of ethical communication in business include:

1. **Honesty**: Provide truthful information, even when it's uncomfortable or potentially damaging in the short term.
2. **Transparency**: Be open about business practices, decisions, and challenges.
3. **Clarity**: Communicate in clear, understandable language, avoiding jargon or obfuscation.
4. **Timeliness**: Share information promptly, especially when it affects stakeholders' decisions or well-being.
5. **Consistency**: Ensure messages align across all channels and levels of the organization.
6. **Respect**: Consider the dignity and rights of all stakeholders in communication.
7. **Responsibility**: Take ownership of mistakes and clearly communicate plans to address them.
8. **Inclusivity**: Ensure all relevant stakeholders are included in communication efforts.

As the proverb states, "The lips of the righteous know what finds favor, but the mouth of the wicked only what is perverse" (Proverbs 10:32). This serves as a reminder of the moral dimension of our communication choices in business.

THE BUSINESS CASE FOR ETHICAL COMMUNICATION

While the moral imperative for ethical communication is clear, it's equally important to recognize its tangible business benefits. Companies that prioritize honest, transparent communication often outperform their less scrupulous counterparts in a variety of ways:

1. Trust and Brand Loyalty

In an era of information overload and heightened skepticism, trust becomes a critical differentiator. Companies known for honest communication build stronger, more resilient relationships with customers.

Consider the case of Patagonia, which has been mentioned repeatedly in our previous chapters. Their transparent communication about their supply chain, environmental impact, and even when they fall short of their own standards has fostered intense customer loyalty and advocacy.

2. Crisis Management and Resilience

Companies with a track record of ethical communication are better positioned to weather crises when they occur.

Johnson & Johnson's handling of the 1982 Tylenol crisis, discussed in earlier chapters, is a case in point. Their quick, honest communication and decisive action not only managed the immediate crisis but also enhanced their long-term reputation.

3. Employee Engagement and Retention

Ethical communication fosters a culture of trust within organizations, leading to higher employee engagement, productivity, and retention.

LinkedIn's transparent approach to internal communications, including regular "All Hands" meetings where employees can ask leadership any question, has contributed to the company's consistently high rankings on "Best Places to Work" lists.

4. Investor Confidence

Transparent, consistent communication with investors can lead to greater confidence, potentially lowering the cost of capital and stabilizing share prices.

Warren Buffett's Berkshire Hathaway is known for its clear, jargon-free annual letters to shareholders. This straightforward communication style has helped build tremendous investor trust and loyalty over decades.

5. Regulatory Compliance and Relationships

Open, ethical communication can help companies stay ahead of regulatory requirements and build more collaborative relationships with regulators.

Unilever's proactive communication about its sustainability efforts and challenges has positioned the company well with regulators and NGOs, often allowing it to shape policy discussions rather than simply react to them.

6. Innovation and Collaboration

A culture of open, honest communication can foster innovation by encouraging the free flow of ideas and constructive feedback.

Google's early culture of openness, including forums where employees could question management decisions, played a critical role in fostering its innovative environment.

As the proverb reminds us, "Truthful lips endure forever, but a lying tongue lasts only a moment" (Proverbs 12:19). In business terms, this speaks to the long-term benefits of consistently ethical communication versus the short-lived gains of deception.

CHALLENGES TO ETHICAL COMMUNICATION

Despite the clear benefits, maintaining ethical communication standards in the modern business environment presents significant challenges:

1. **Short-Term Pressures:** The demand for positive quarterly results can lead companies to downplay negative information or overstate positive developments.

2. **Complex Information:** In industries that deal with complex technical or financial information, there can

be a temptation to hide unfavorable data in jargon or complicated presentations.

3. **Legal Constraints**: Legal considerations, particularly for publicly traded companies, can sometimes conflict with the desire for full transparency.

4. **Competitive Concerns**: Companies may be reluctant to communicate openly about strategies or challenges for fear of giving competitors an advantage.

5. **Rapid Information Flow**: In the age of social media and 24/7 news cycles, organizations must balance the need for quick responses with the need for accuracy and thoughtfulness.

6. **Cultural Differences**: Global organizations must navigate different cultural norms and expectations around communication, which can sometimes conflict with universal ethical standards.

As the proverb warns, "The one who has knowledge uses words with restraint, and whoever has understanding is even-tempered" (Proverbs 17:27). This wisdom reminds us of the need for careful, considered communication, especially in challenging situations.

STRATEGIES FOR FOSTERING ETHICAL COMMUNICATION

Creating and maintaining a culture of ethical communication requires conscious effort and ongoing commitment. Here are key strategies for promoting truthful, transparent communication in business:

1. **Lead by Example**: Leaders must consistently demonstrate a commitment to ethical communication in their words and actions.

   As the proverb states, "A ruler who listens to lies, all his officials become wicked" (Proverbs 29:12). This underscores the cascading effect of leadership behavior on organizational culture.

2. **Develop Clear Communication Policies**: Establish and communicate clear guidelines for ethical communication at all levels of the organization.

3. **Foster a Speak-Up Culture**: Create an environment where employees feel safe to raise concerns and share information without fear of retaliation.

4. **Prioritize Transparency**: Make transparency a core value, consistently sharing both positive and negative information with stakeholders.

5. **Invest in Communication Training**: Provide ongoing training to employees at all levels on effective and ethical communication practices.

6. **Utilize Clear, Accessible Language**: Strive to communicate complex information in clear, understandable terms, avoiding unnecessary jargon or obfuscation.

7. **Implement Strong Fact-Checking Processes**: Establish rigorous fact-checking procedures to ensure the accuracy of all external communications.

8. **Encourage Two-Way Communication**: Create
   channels for stakeholder feedback and demonstrate a
   willingness to listen and respond.

9. **Plan for Crises**: Develop crisis communication plans
   that prioritize quick, honest, and transparent
   responses.

10. **Regularly Assess Communication Practices**:
    Periodically review communications practices to
    ensure they are consistent with ethical standards and
    corporate values.

As the proverb advises, "The heart of the righteous weighs its answers, but the mouth of the wicked gushes evil" (Proverbs 15:28). This wisdom emphasizes the importance of thoughtful, considered communication rather than hasty or self-serving responses.

THE PATH FORWARD

As the sun dipped below the horizon, casting long shadows across her office, Rachel Thompson sat at her desk, the weight of the day's events bearing down on her. She'd won the battle in the boardroom, but the war for MediCore's reputation and future had just begun.

Her computer screen glowed with the draft of the press release that would rock the pharmaceutical world. It was clear, concise, and, above all, honest. There was no spin nor evasion, just the unvarnished truth about the side effects of her medication and her plan to address the problem.

Rachel's finger hovered over the send button. Once this went out, there would be no turning back. The stock would plummet, the media would descend like vultures, and lawsuits would surely follow.

But as she hesitated, her grandmother's voice echoed in her mind, quoting another proverb: "Whoever walks in integrity walks securely, but whoever takes crooked paths will be found out" (Proverbs 10:9).

Taking a deep breath, Rachel clicked "Send. As the email whirred away, she felt a strange mixture of dread and relief. The road ahead would be difficult, but she knew in her heart it was the right one.

In the days and weeks that followed, MediCore weathered a storm of media scrutiny and market volatility. But out of the chaos, something unexpected began to emerge. Patients and doctors praised the company's honesty. Ethicists held it up as an example of corporate responsibility. Even some investors, after the initial shock, began to express confidence in the company's long-term prospects, impressed by its commitment to transparency.

Six months later, Rachel stood before the board again, this time with a very different report to deliver. "Ladies and gentlemen," she began, a smile playing on her lips, "I am pleased to report that our trust ratings have reached an all-time high. Our sales, after an initial dip, have stabilized and are beginning to rise again. And perhaps most importantly, we've set a new standard for ethical communications in our industry.

Dr. Chen, who had been her staunchest ally during the turbulent times, nodded in agreement. "Ms. Thompson, when you first proposed this strategy, I thought you were either a genius or crazy. Now I see that you were just smart. You've taught us all a valuable lesson about the power of truth in business.

As the meeting adjourned, Rachel felt a sense of pride and purpose she'd never experienced before. In a world often clouded by corporate doublespeak and evasion, MediCore had chosen the path of radical honesty and emerged stronger for it.

In boardrooms and offices worldwide, similar decisions about communication ethics are made every day. As companies grapple with the pressures of a hyper-connected, information-rich global economy, the wisdom encapsulated in ancient proverbs provides a timeless guide. The challenges may be new, but the principles of ethical communication remain constant:

> *"The Lord detests lying lips, but he delights in people who are trustworthy." (Proverbs 12:22)*

> *"Truthful lips endure forever, but a lying tongue lasts only a moment." (Proverbs 12:19)*

> *"Whoever walks in integrity walks securely, but whoever takes crooked paths will be found out." (Proverbs 10:9)*

These proverbs remind us that in business, as in life, our words have power. They can build or destroy, heal or harm, inspire trust, or sow suspicion. In an age when information travels at the speed of light, and corporate misdeeds can be exposed with a single tweet, the value of consistent, ethical communication cannot be overstated.

The road to ethical communication is rarely the easiest. It requires courage to speak uncomfortable truths, wisdom to navigate complex situations, and discipline to maintain consistency across all touchpoints. But as we've seen, it leads not only to sustainable success but also to a deeper, more fulfilling way of doing business.

As we continue our exploration of ancient wisdom in modern business, let these principles of ethical communication guide us. In the chapters to come, we will explore related themes- the power of ethical leadership, the importance of corporate social responsibility, and the role of business in shaping societal values. Throughout, the lessons learned about the transformative power of truth-telling in business will serve as a foundation, a constant reminder of the enduring value of ethical communication.

Let us move forward, guided by the wisdom of the ages, as we continue to explore the rich intersection of ancient principles and modern business practices. In doing so, we can build organizations that are not only financially successful but also make a positive contribution to our world - fostering trust, inspiring confidence, and setting a standard of integrity that elevates the entire business landscape.

NINE

ETHICAL INNOVATION - CREATING VALUE RESPONSIBLY

"*The plans of the diligent lead to profit as surely as haste leads to poverty.*" - *Proverbs 21:5*

The cavernous research lab at EcoTech Innovations buzzed with energy. Dr. Samantha Patel stood in front of a holographic display, her eyes darting between complex molecular structures floating in the air. Her team had just made a breakthrough in sustainable energy storage, a technology with the potential to revolutionize the use of renewable energy worldwide.

But as Samantha's excitement peaked, a nagging doubt crept into her mind. The new technology relied on a rare mineral whose extraction had a devastating environmental impact. Was the quest for clean energy worth the environmental cost of its production?

A knock at the door interrupted her thoughts. "Come in," she called, not looking up from the display.

Marcus Chen, EcoTech's ambitious CEO, strode into the lab, his eyes bright with anticipation. "Dr. Patel, I hear congratulations are in order. This breakthrough could put us years ahead of the competition."

Samantha turned and met Marcus's eager gaze. "Thank you, Marcus. The team has done an incredible job. But... there's something we need to discuss."

Marcus' smile faltered. "What is it? Don't tell me there's a problem with the prototype?"

"Not with the prototype itself," Samantha explained, gesturing to the holographic display. "The technology works beautifully. However, the key component requires a mineral that's extremely difficult to extract ethically. The environmental impact of mining it could potentially negate the benefits of the clean energy it enables."

Marcus' brow furrowed. "But surely the long-term benefits outweigh the short-term costs? This could be the key to global adoption of renewable energy."

Samantha shook her head. "It's not that simple. We'd be solving one environmental problem by creating another. That goes against everything EcoTech stands for.

A tense silence filled the lab. Marcus paced, his mind clearly racing. "We've invested millions in this research, Samantha. The board expects results. We can't slow down now."

Samantha stood firm. "I understand the pressure, Marcus. However, as scientists and innovators, we have a responsibility to consider the full impact of our work. There's an old saying that my father, a small-town inventor, used to quote: 'The plans of the diligent lead to profit as surely as haste leads to poverty.' We must be careful not only in our scientific process but also in our ethical considerations.

Marcus' expression softened, a mixture of frustration and respect crossing his face. "You're right, of course. But what do you suggest we do? Abandon the project altogether?"

Samantha turned back to the holographic display, her mind already formulating a new plan. "Not give up, pivot. We've made significant advances in energy storage technology. Let's use that knowledge to explore alternative materials, ones we can source responsibly."

She manipulated the hologram, bringing up a new set of molecular structures. "I already have some ideas. It may take longer, and the path isn't as clear, but if we succeed, we'll have a truly sustainable solution. One that aligns with our values and our mission."

Marcus studied the new display, his initial skepticism giving way to curiosity. "It's a risk," he mused. "But then again, true innovation always is." He turned to Samantha, a new determination in his eyes. "All right, Dr. Patel. You have my support. Let's show the world what ethical innovation looks like.

As Marcus left the lab, Samantha felt a weight lift from her shoulders. The road ahead would be challenging, but in her heart, she knew it was the right one. In a world often driven by short-term gains and quick fixes, a commitment to responsible innovation could be its greatest differentiator.

THE ESSENCE OF ETHICAL INNOVATION IN BUSINESS

In the rapidly evolving landscape of modern business, innovation is a key driver of growth and competitive advantage.

However, ethical innovation goes beyond mere novelty or technological advancement; it encompasses a holistic approach to responsible value creation that considers the broader implications and impacts of new ideas and technologies.

As another proverb wisely counsels, "The wise prevail through great power, and those who have knowledge muster their strength" (Proverbs 24:5). In a business context, this speaks to the power of combining innovation with ethical considerations and foresight.

Key aspects of ethical innovation include:

1. **Responsible Development**: Consider the potential consequences and impacts of innovations throughout the development process.
2. **Sustainability**: Prioritize innovations that contribute to long-term environmental and social sustainability.
3. **Inclusivity**: Ensure that innovation benefits a wide range of stakeholders, not just a privileged few.
4. **Transparency**: Be open about the processes, materials, and potential impacts of innovations.
5. **Safety and Well-being**: Prioritize the safety and well-being of users, workers, and communities affected by innovations.
6. **Ethical Sourcing**: Ensure that materials and resources used in innovation are sourced responsibly and ethically.
7. **Long-term Thinking**: Consider the long-term impact of innovations, not just the immediate benefits or profits.
8. **Cultural Sensitivity**: Respect diverse cultural values and norms when developing and implementing innovations.

As the proverb states, "The simple inherit folly, but the prudent are crowned with knowledge" (Proverbs 14:18). This serves as a reminder of the importance of thoughtful, responsible innovation rather than hasty or short-sighted development.

THE BUSINESS CASE FOR ETHICAL INNOVATION

While the moral imperative for ethical innovation is clear, it's equally important to recognize its tangible business benefits. Companies that prioritize responsible innovation often outperform their less scrupulous counterparts in a variety of ways:

1. Enhanced Brand Reputation and Customer Loyalty

In an era of heightened consumer awareness, companies known for ethical innovation can build stronger brands and foster deeper customer loyalty.

Consider the case of Patagonia, a company mentioned throughout the previous chapters. Their innovations in sustainable materials and ethical production processes have not only reduced their environmental impact but also strengthened their brand and customer base.

2. Increased Market Opportunities

Ethical innovation often opens up new markets and customer segments, particularly among socially conscious consumers and in developing countries.

Unilever's Sustainable Living Plan, which drives the company to develop more environmentally and socially responsible products, has opened new markets and driven growth in emerging markets.

3. Improved Risk Management

By considering ethical implications early in the innovation process, companies can avoid potential pitfalls and scandals that could damage their reputations and bottom lines.

Toyota's early investment in hybrid technology, driven by environmental concerns, not only led to the successful Prius but also protected the company from the full impact of rising fuel prices and increasing emissions regulations.

4. Attraction and Retention of Top Talent

Companies known for ethical innovation are often more attractive to top talent, especially among younger generations who prioritize working for socially responsible organizations.

Google's "20% time" policy, which allowed employees to spend a portion of their work time on projects they were passionate about, not only resulted in innovative products but also helped attract and retain top talent in the competitive technology industry.

5. Long-term Sustainability and Profitability

Ethical innovation often leads to more sustainable business models and long-term profitability, even if it requires more upfront investment.

Interface, a carpet manufacturer, transformed its business model to focus on sustainability, resulting in innovative products and processes that not only reduced environmental impact but also improved profitability.

6. Positive Societal Impact

Ethical innovation can have a significant positive impact on society, enhancing a company's social license to operate and creating goodwill among stakeholders.

Tesla's innovations in electric vehicles and renewable energy storage have not only built a valuable company but also accelerated the global transition to sustainable transportation and energy.

As the proverb reminds us, "A good name is more desirable than great riches; to be esteemed is better than silver or gold" (Proverbs 22:1). In business terms, this speaks to the long-term value of building a reputation for ethical innovation, which can outweigh short-term financial gains.

CHALLENGES TO ETHICAL INNOVATION

Despite its clear benefits, maintaining a commitment to ethical innovation in the modern business environment presents significant challenges:

1. **Short-term Profit Pressures**: The demand for rapid return on investment can discourage the often longer development cycles required for ethical innovation.

2. **Competitive Pressures**: In fast-moving industries, there can be a temptation to cut ethical corners to beat competitors to market.

3. **Complexity of Ethical Considerations**: The ethical implications of new technologies can be complex and difficult to predict, making it difficult to make fully informed decisions.

4. **Resource Constraints**: Ethical innovation often requires additional resources, which can be a challenge for companies with limited budgets.

5. **Regulatory Uncertainty**: Rapidly evolving technologies often outpace regulatory frameworks, creating uncertainty about future compliance requirements.

6. **Stakeholder Alignment**: Balancing the diverse and sometimes conflicting interests of different stakeholders in the innovation process can be challenging.

As the proverb warns, "The greedy stir up conflict, but those who trust in the Lord will prosper" (Proverbs 28:25). This wisdom reminds us of the potential pitfalls of pursuing innovation purely for profit, without ethical considerations.

STRATEGIES FOR FOSTERING ETHICAL INNOVATION

Creating and maintaining a culture of ethical innovation requires deliberate effort and ongoing commitment. Here are key strategies for promoting responsible innovation in business:

1. **Embed Ethics in the Innovation Process**: Integrate ethical considerations into every stage of the innovation process, from ideation to implementation.

   As the proverb states, "Commit to the Lord whatever you do, and he will establish your plans" (Proverbs 16:3). This underscores the importance of grounding our innovation efforts in solid ethical principles.

2. **Cultivate Diverse Perspectives**: Encourage diversity on innovation teams to bring a wide range of perspectives to ethical considerations.

3. **Implement Ethical Impact Assessments**: Develop and use tools to assess the potential ethical impact of innovations before they are developed or released.

4. **Foster a Culture of Responsibility**: Create an organizational culture where employees feel empowered and accountable for considering the ethical implications of their work.

5. **Engage Stakeholders**: Actively engage with diverse stakeholders to understand their perspectives and concerns about innovation.

6. **Invest in Long-term Research**: Dedicate resources to long-term research that prioritizes ethical and sustainable solutions, even if the payoff isn't immediate.

7. **Collaborate for Ethical Solutions**: Partnering with other organizations, including competitors, when appropriate, to solve complex ethical challenges in innovation.

8. **Prioritize Transparency**: Be open about innovation processes, including ethical challenges and how they're being addressed.

9. **Educate and Train**: Conduct ongoing education and training on ethical innovation principles and practices.

10. **Lead by Example**: Leaders must consistently demonstrate a commitment to ethical innovation in their decisions and actions.

As the proverb advises, "The path of the righteous is like the morning sun, shining ever brighter till the full light of day" (Proverbs 4:18). This wisdom emphasizes the gradual but powerful impact of consistent commitment to ethical practices in innovation.

THE PATH FORWARD

Samantha Patel stood in front of her team as the sun dipped below the horizon, casting a warm glow through the lab windows. The past six months had been a whirlwind of new research, ethical debates, and relentless problem-solving. But now, as she looked into the faces of her colleagues, she saw the same mix of exhaustion and excitement she felt herself.

"Team," she began, her voice steady with determination, "I want to thank each of you for your incredible work. When we decided to redirect our research to find a more ethical solution, I know many of you had doubts. It wasn't the easy way, but it was the right way.

She gestured to the holographic display behind her, where a new molecular structure was slowly rotating. "What we've achieved here is more than a technological breakthrough. It's a testament to what's possible when we commit to innovation that aligns with our values.

Marcus Chen, who had been silently observing from the back of the room, stepped forward. "Dr. Patel is being modest," he said, a proud smile on his face. "What this team has accomplished is nothing short of revolutionary. Not only have we created an energy storage solution that is more efficient than our original design, but we've done it using materials that are abundant and ethically sourced."

A wave of pride swept through the room. Samantha continued, "Our journey is not over. We still have challenges ahead as we move toward production and launch. But we've proven that ethical innovation is not just a lofty ideal- it's a practical, achievable goal that can drive our business forward.

As the team dispersed, energized by the progress and the road ahead, Samantha found herself alone with Marcus.

"You were right," he said softly. "Taking the time to do this right, to innovate ethically - it's not just good for our conscience, it's good for our business. We're not just creating a product; we're setting a new standard for our entire industry."

Samantha nodded, a mixture of satisfaction and determination in her eyes. "It's like the saying my father used to quote: 'The plans of the industrious lead to profit as surely as haste leads to poverty. We've been diligent - in our science, in our ethics, in our commitment to our values. And I believe that diligence will lead us to success beyond what we originally imagined.

Both leaders left the lab with a renewed sense of purpose. In a world often driven by the race to be first, they had chosen to prioritize being right ethically, environmentally, and economically. It was a choice that would shape not only EcoTech's future but potentially the future of sustainable energy worldwide.

In research labs, boardrooms, and offices around the world, similar choices about ethical innovation are made every day. As companies grapple with the pressures of a rapidly changing technological landscape and mounting global challenges, the wisdom encapsulated in ancient proverbs provides a timeless guide. The challenges may be new, but the principles of responsible innovation remain constant:

> *"The plans of the diligent lead to profit as surely as haste leads to poverty." (Proverbs 21:5).*

> *"The wise prevail through great power, and those who have knowledge muster their strength." (Proverbs 24:5).*

> *"A good name is more desirable than great riches; to be esteemed is better than silver or gold." (Proverbs 22:1)*

These proverbs remind us that in business, as in life, true success comes not just from what we create but also from how we create it. At a time when technological advances can have far-reaching and sometimes unforeseen consequences, the importance of ethical innovation cannot be overstated.

The road to ethical innovation is rarely the easiest. It requires courage to challenge conventional thinking, wisdom to antici-pate potential impacts, and perseverance to pursue responsible solutions even when they aren't the fastest or cheapest options. But as we've seen, it's a path that leads not only to sustainable success but also to a deeper, more fulfilling way of doing business.

As we continue our exploration of ancient wisdom in modern business, let these principles of ethical innovation guide us. In the chapters to come, we will explore related themes, such as the power of purpose-driven business, the importance of stew-ardship in leadership, and the role of business in solving global challenges. Throughout, the lessons learned about the trans-formative power of responsible innovation will serve as a foun-dation, a constant reminder of the enduring value of ethical value creation.

Let us move forward, guided by the wisdom of the ages, as we continue to explore the rich intersection of ancient principles and modern business practices. In doing so, we can build orga-nizations that not only succeed financially but also make a positive contribution to our world-driving progress, solving problems, and setting a standard of responsible innovation that elevates the entire business landscape.

TEN
ETHICAL CONFLICT RESOLUTION - WISDOM IN DISPUTES

" Starting a quarrel is like breaching a dam; so drop the matter before a dispute breaks out." - Proverbs 17:14

The boardroom of Global Synergy Corporation buzzed with excitement. Jack Donovan, CEO of the company's North American division, sat on one side of the polished mahogany table. Across from him, Elena Petrovna, head of European operations, leaned forward, her eyes flashing with barely contained frustration.

Between them, looking increasingly uncomfortable, sat Amelia Wu, the newly appointed Chief Ethics Officer. Her first major task in that role had landed her in the middle of a brewing storm.

"This is absurd," Jack snapped, his voice rising. "We can't possibly comply with these new European regulations without jeopardizing our entire North American strategy. Elena, your team needs to push back harder against these bureaucrats!"

Elena's jaw clenched. "And risk massive fines or even losing our license to operate? The rules are clear, Jack. It's your outdated practices that put us all at risk."

As the argument escalated, Amelia's mind raced. She'd been brought in to help navigate exactly this kind of ethical mine-field, but the stakes were higher than she'd anticipated. Global Synergy's entire global strategy hung in the balance.

Taking a deep breath, Amelia raised her hand, cutting through the heated exchange. "If I may," she began, her voice calm but firm, "I think we're approaching this from the wrong angle."

Both executives turned to her, surprised and with a hint of skepticism in their eyes.

"There's an old proverb my mentor used to quote," Amelia continued. "'Starting a quarrel is like breaching a dam, so drop the matter before a dispute breaks out.' Right now, we're in danger of breaching that dam. Instead of arguing over whose approach is right or wrong, let's take a step back and look at the underlying interests and values at play here."

Jack leaned back and crossed his arms. "And how do you propose we do that, Ms. Wu?"

Amelia stood and walked to the whiteboard at the end of the room. "Let's start by clearly articulating what each department needs, what constraints we face, and most importantly, what ethical principles should guide our decision. Then we can work together to find a solution that addresses all of these concerns."

As she began to write, Elena and Jack exchanged glances. The tension in the room began to dissipate, replaced by a cautious curiosity.

"All right, Amelia," Elena said, a note of respect in her voice. "Let's try it your way."

Over the next few hours, under Amelia's guidance, the conversation changed. Instead of pointing fingers, the leaders began to explore common ground. As they delved into the ethical implications of their decisions, new possibilities emerged.

By the time the meeting adjourned, a framework for a new global strategy had taken shape that not only complied with regulations but also set a new standard for ethical business practices throughout the company's operations.

As Jack and Elena left the boardroom, their former animosity was replaced by a shared sense of purpose, and Amelia felt a wave of relief and accomplishment wash over her. In a world where corporate conflicts often escalate into legal battles or public relations nightmares, the power of ethical conflict resolution could be transformative.

She recalled another proverb: "The quiet words of the wise are more to be heeded than the shouts of a ruler in folly" (Ecclesiastes 9:17). In the complex landscape of modern business, wisdom and ethical leadership can indeed speak louder than loudest arguments.

THE ESSENCE OF ETHICAL CONFLICT RESOLUTION IN BUSINESS

In the dynamic and often high-pressure world of business, conflict is inevitable. Ethical conflict resolution, however, goes beyond mere compromise or win-lose outcomes. It seeks to resolve disputes in a way that upholds moral principles, preserves relationships, and ultimately strengthens the organization.

As another proverb wisely counsels, "A hot-tempered person stirs up conflict, but the one who is patient calms a quarrel" (Proverbs 15:18). In a business context, this speaks to the importance of approaching conflicts with a cool head and a commitment to finding ethical solutions.

Key aspects of ethical conflict resolution include:

1. **Fairness**: Ensure that all parties have an equal opportunity to present their perspectives and concerns.
2. **Transparency**: Be open and honest about the issues at hand, including any underlying factors or constraints.
3. **Respect**: Treat all parties with dignity, regardless of their position or the nature of the conflict.
4. **Objectivity**: Try to look at the situation with an open mind and consider all relevant factors.
5. **Collaboration**: Encourage the parties to work together to find mutually beneficial solutions.
6. **Ethical Consideration**: Evaluate potential resolutions against ethical standards and organizational values.
7. **Long-term Perspective**: Consider the long-term impact of decisions, not just the immediate results.
8. **Confidentiality**: Respect the privacy of those involved while being transparent about the process.

As the proverb states, "The purposes of a person's heart are deep waters, but one who has insight draws them out" (Proverbs 20:5). This serves as a reminder of the importance of understanding the underlying motivations and concerns in any conflict situation.

THE BUSINESS CASE FOR ETHICAL CONFLICT RESOLUTION

While the moral imperative for ethical conflict resolution is clear, it's equally important to recognize its tangible business benefits. Organizations that manage conflict ethically often outperform their less scrupulous counterparts in a variety of ways:

1. Improved Organizational Culture

Ethical conflict resolution fosters a culture of trust and open communication, which leads to higher employee satisfaction and engagement.

Consider the case of Patagonia, a company we've mentioned in previous chapters. Their commitment to addressing conflicts transparently and ethically, even when it means challenging their own practices, has contributed to a strong, values-driven culture that attracts and retains top talent.

2. Enhanced Decision Making

Ethical conflict resolution often leads to more robust, well-considered decisions by encouraging diverse perspectives and collaborative problem-solving.

Google's early culture of open debate and ethical discussion, exemplified by its "Don't be evil" motto, contributed to innovative problem-solving and decision-making processes.

3. Stronger Stakeholder Relationships

Organizations with a reputation for ethical conflict management often enjoy stronger, more resilient relationships with employees, customers, suppliers, and other stakeholders.

Johnson & Johnson's handling of the 1982 Tylenol crisis, which we've discussed in earlier chapters, demonstrates how ethical conflict resolution can strengthen stakeholder trust even in the face of significant challenges.

4. Reduced Legal and Reputational Risks

Ethical conflict resolution can often prevent disputes from escalating into costly litigation or public relations crises.

Starbucks' response to a racial bias incident in 2018, which included closing stores for racial bias training and implementing new policies, shows how ethical conflict resolution can mitigate reputational damage and drive positive change.

5. Increased Innovation and Adaptability

A culture that resolves conflict ethically is often more open to diverse ideas and better able to adapt to changing circumstances.

Toyota's approach to conflict resolution, rooted in its principle of "respect for people," has contributed to its ability to continuously improve and innovate in its manufacturing processes.

6. Improved Bottom Line

While ethical conflict resolution sometimes involves short-term costs, it often results in long-term financial benefits through improved efficiency, reduced turnover, and stronger stakeholder relationships.

As the proverb reminds us, "Better a little with righteousness than much gain with injustice" (Proverbs 16:8). In business terms, this speaks to the long-term value of ethical practices, including in conflict resolution, which can outweigh short-term gains achieved through less ethical means.

CHALLENGES TO ETHICAL CONFLICT RESOLUTION

Despite its clear benefits, maintaining a commitment to ethical conflict resolution in the modern business environment presents significant challenges:

1. **Power Imbalances**: In organizations with strong hierarchies, there may be a temptation for those in positions of power to impose solutions rather than engage in ethical conflict resolution processes.

2. **Time Pressures**: In fast-paced business environments, there can be a push for quick solutions, potentially at the expense of more thoughtful, ethical approaches.

3. **Cultural Differences**: In global organizations, different cultural norms and expectations around conflict and resolution can complicate the process.

4. **Emotional Intensity**: Business conflicts often involve high stakes and strong emotions, which can

make it difficult to maintain an ethical, rational approach.

5. **Legal Considerations**: The threat of legal action can sometimes overshadow efforts at ethical resolution, pushing parties toward adversarial rather than collaborative approaches.

6. **Short-term Thinking**: Pressure for immediate results can lead to conflict resolutions that prioritize short-term gains over long-term ethical considerations.

As the proverb warns, "Fools show their annoyance at once, but the prudent overlook an insult" (Proverbs 12:16). This wisdom reminds us of the importance of maintaining composure and a long-term perspective in the face of conflicts.

STRATEGIES FOR FOSTERING ETHICAL CONFLICT RESOLUTION

Creating and maintaining a culture of ethical conflict resolution requires deliberate effort and ongoing commitment. Here are key strategies for promoting ethical approaches to conflict in business:

1. **Establish Clear Ethical Guidelines**: Develop and communicate clear ethical principles to guide conflict resolution processes throughout the organization.

As the proverb states, "The way of fools seems right to them, but the wise listen to advice" (Proverbs 12:15). This underscores the importance of establishing wise, ethical guidelines rather than relying on individual judgment alone.

2. **Promote Open Communication**: Foster an organizational culture where people feel safe to raise concerns and engage in constructive dialogue about conflict.

3. **Provide Conflict Resolution Training**: Offer ongoing training in ethical conflict resolution techniques to employees at all levels of the organization.

4. **Use Neutral Third Parties**: When appropriate, engage neutral mediators or facilitators to help resolve complex or sensitive conflicts.

5. **Emphasize Common Ground**: Encourage parties to focus on shared interests and values rather than entrenched positions.

6. **Practice Active Listening**: Train leaders and employees in active listening techniques to ensure that all perspectives are fully understood.

7. **Consider All Stakeholders**: When resolving conflicts, consider the potential impact on all stakeholders, not just the parties directly involved.

8. **Implement Fair Processes**: Ensure that conflict resolution processes are transparent, consistent, and perceived as fair by all parties.

9. **Learn from Conflicts**: Use conflict as an opportunity for organizational learning and improvement, not as an event to be avoided or hidden.

10. **Lead by Example**: Leaders must consistently demonstrate their commitment to ethical conflict resolution in their own behavior and decisions.

As the proverb advises, "Plans fail for lack of counsel, but with many advisers, they succeed" (Proverbs 15:22). This wisdom emphasizes the importance of seeking diverse perspectives and collaborative approaches in resolving conflicts.

THE PATH FORWARD

As the sun dipped below the horizon, casting long shadows across her office, Amelia Wu sat at her desk, reflecting on the day's events. The conflict between Jack and Elena had been resolved, but she knew it was only the beginning. Transforming Global Synergy's approach to conflict resolution would be a long-term process.

She pulled out a notebook and began to sketch out a plan. First, a company-wide assessment of current conflict resolution practices. Then, the development of a comprehensive ethical framework for handling disputes. Finally, a series of training programs to embed these principles throughout the organization.

As she worked, Amelia recalled another proverb: "As iron sharpens iron, so one person sharpens another" (Proverbs 27:17). She smiled, realizing that conflicts, when approached ethically, could indeed be opportunities for growth and improvement.

A knock at her door interrupted her thoughts. She looked up to see Jack and Elena enter, both wearing expressions of newfound respect.

"Amelia," Jack began, "Elena and I have been talking. We want to thank you for today. Your approach... it has opened our eyes to a new way of thinking about our challenges."

Elena nodded in agreement. "We realized that our conflict was never really about policies or strategies. It was about our shared commitment to the success of this company and our different ideas about how to achieve it."

Amelia felt a surge of pride and hope. "I'm glad I could help. But this is just the beginning. We have an opportunity here to transform the way our entire organization approaches conflict and challenge.

Jack and Elena exchanged glances, then turned back to Amelia with determined expressions. "We're on board," Jack said. "Whatever it takes to make this happen, you have our full support."

As they left her office, Amelia returned to her plans with renewed energy. In a world where corporate conflicts often escalate into destructive battles, the power of ethical conflict resolution could be truly transformative. It wasn't just about solving immediate problems; it was about building a stronger, more resilient organization for the long term.

Conflict occurs every day in boardrooms, offices, and workplaces around the world. As organizations grapple with competing interests, differing perspectives, and complex ethical dilemmas, the wisdom encapsulated in ancient proverbs provides a timeless guide. The nature of conflicts may change, but the principles of ethical resolution remain constant:

"Starting a quarrel is like breaching a dam; so drop the matter before a dispute breaks out." (Proverbs 17:14).

"A hot-tempered person stirs up conflict, but the one who is patient calms a quarrel." (Proverbs 15:18)

"As iron sharpens iron, so one person sharpens another." (Proverbs 27:17)

These proverbs remind us that in business, as in life, conflicts are not inherently destructive. When approached with wisdom, patience, and ethical consideration, they can be opportunities for growth, innovation, and strengthening relationships.

The path of ethical conflict resolution is rarely the easiest. It requires courage to confront issues openly, wisdom to see beyond immediate interests, and patience to work through complex problems. But as we've seen, it leads not only to better resolutions but also to stronger, more resilient organizations.

As we continue our exploration of ancient wisdom in modern business, let these principles of ethical conflict resolution guide us. In the chapters to come, we will delve deeper into related themes – the power of ethical leadership in crisis, the importance of building trust across diverse teams, and the role of businesses in promoting social harmony. Through it all, the lessons learned about the transformative power of ethical conflict resolution will serve as a foundation, a constant reminder of the enduring value of addressing disputes with wisdom and integrity.

Let us move forward, guided by the wisdom of the ages, as we continue to explore the rich intersection of ancient principles and modern business practices. In doing so, we can build organizations that not only successfully navigate conflicts but also use them as catalysts for positive change—fostering cultures of trust, collaboration, and ethical decision-making that elevate the entire business landscape.

ELEVEN

ENVIRONMENTAL STEWARDSHIP - ETHICAL RESOURCE MANAGEMENT

"The righteous care for the needs of their animals, but the kindest acts of the wicked are cruel." - Proverbs 12:10

The vast expanse of the Amazon rainforest stretched out before Lucas Alvarez, CEO of GreenHarvest Corporation. From the helicopter window, the lush canopy seemed endless, a sea of green teeming with life. But Lucas knew better. With each passing year, more of this vital ecosystem disappeared, cleared for agriculture and industry.

As the helicopter touched down at the site of GreenHarvest's newest plantation, Lucas steeled himself for the task ahead. His company was at a crossroads. Demand for its ethically sourced palm oil had skyrocketed, creating an unprecedented opportunity for growth. But expansion meant clearing more rainforest, a move at odds with the company's stated commitment to sustainability.

GreenHarvest's chief sustainability officer, Maria Santiago, met Lucas as he disembarked. A look of concern replaced her usual warm smile. "Lucas, we need to talk," she said, her voice barely audible over the whir of the helicopter blades.

As they walked toward the plantation's main building, Maria launched into her report. "The Environmental Impact Assessment has come back. If we go ahead with the expansion as planned, we'll be destroying critical habitat for several endangered species. Not to mention the carbon impact..."

Lucas held up a hand, silencing her. He'd heard it all before. "Maria, I understand your concerns. But we have shareholders to answer to. This expansion could double our profits in five years.

Maria's eyes flashed with determination. "And what about our responsibility to the planet? To future generations? Lucas, there's an old proverb my grandmother used to quote: 'The righteous care for the needs of their animals, but the kindest acts of the wicked are cruel.' If we go ahead with this expansion, how are we any different than the corporations we've criticized for putting profit before the health of the planet?"

Her words hit Lucas like a physical blow. He'd founded Green-Harvest with a vision to prove that it was possible to run a profitable business while being a responsible steward of the environment. Had he lost sight of that in the pursuit of profit?

As they reached the plantation's observation deck, Lucas looked out over the fields his company had cultivated. Beyond them lay the pristine rainforest, a vibrant ecosystem that had taken millennia to evolve. At that moment, the weight of his decision pressed down on him like a physical force.

"You're right, Maria," he said quietly. "We have lost our way. But it's not too late to change course. I need you to draw up a new expansion plan. One that prioritizes conservation and reforestation, even if it means slower growth.

Maria's eyes widened in surprise, then sparkled with renewed purpose. "I'll get right on it. Lucas, this could set a new standard for ethical resource management in our industry."

As Maria rushed off to begin work on the new plan, Lucas remained on the observation deck, his mind racing with possibilities. He recalled another proverb: "A good person leaves an inheritance for their children's children, but a sinner's wealth is stored up for the righteous" (Proverbs 13:22).

At that moment, Lucas realized that the true legacy he wanted to leave wasn't measured in profits or market share but in preserving the natural world for generations to come. The road ahead would be challenging, but he knew in his heart it was the right one. In a world often driven by short-term profits and resource exploitation, GreenHarvest could become a beacon of ethical environmental stewardship.

THE ESSENCE OF ENVIRONMENTAL STEWARDSHIP IN BUSINESS

In today's business environment, where resource scarcity and environmental degradation pose increasing challenges, environmental stewardship has evolved from a peripheral concern to a central tenet of ethical business practice. It encompasses not only compliance with environmental regulations but also a proactive approach to preserving and nurturing the natural world on which all businesses ultimately depend.

As another proverb wisely counsels, "The prudent see danger and take refuge, but the simple keep going and pay the penalty" (Proverbs 22:3). In a business context, this speaks to the foresight required to recognize environmental risks and take decisive action to mitigate them.

Key aspects of environmental stewardship include:

1. **Resource Conservation**: Use natural resources efficiently and sparingly, recognizing their finite nature.
2. **Pollution Prevention**: Minimize or eliminate harmful emissions and waste in all business operations.
3. **Biodiversity Protection**: Safeguard ecosystems and the diversity of life they support.
4. **Climate Change Mitigation**: Reduce greenhouse gas emissions and support climate resilience efforts.
5. **Circular Economy Practices**: Design products and processes to eliminate waste and maximize resource reuse.
6. **Sustainable Supply Chains**: Ensure environmental responsibility extends throughout the entire supply chain.
7. **Environmental Education**: Raise awareness and promote environmental responsibility among employees and stakeholders.
8. **Restoration and Regeneration**: Actively work to restore damaged ecosystems and regenerate natural resources.

As the proverb states, "The earth is the Lord's, and everything in it, the world, and all who live in it" (Psalm 24:1). This serves as a reminder of the profound responsibility we bear as stewards of the natural world.

THE BUSINESS CASE FOR ENVIRONMENTAL STEWARDSHIP

While the moral imperative for environmental stewardship is clear, it's equally important to recognize its tangible business benefits. Companies that prioritize ethical resource management often outperform their less environmentally responsible counterparts in a variety of ways:

1. Cost Savings and Efficiency

Environmentally responsible practices often result in significant cost savings through reduced resource use and improved efficiency.

Consider the case of Unilever, whose Sustainable Living Plan has not only reduced its environmental impact but also generated more than $1 billion in cost savings through efficiency measures and resource conservation.

2. Innovation and New Market Opportunities

Environmental challenges often drive innovation, leading to new products, services, and markets.

Tesla's focus on electric vehicles and sustainable energy solutions has not only disrupted the automotive industry but also opened up new markets in energy storage and solar power.

3. Enhanced Brand Reputation and Customer Loyalty

Companies with strong environmental stewardship often enjoy increased brand equity and customer loyalty.

We've mentioned Patagonia in previous chapters. This company has built a fiercely loyal customer base, in large part because of its commitment to environmental responsibility and transparency about its environmental impact.

4. Improved Risk Management

Proactive environmental management can help companies anticipate and mitigate risks associated with resource scarcity, regulatory changes, and climate impacts.

Walmart's efforts to improve energy efficiency and reduce greenhouse gas emissions across its operations and supply chain have not only reduced costs but also improved its resilience to energy price volatility and potential carbon regulations.

5. Attraction and Retention of Talent

Companies with strong environmental credentials often find it easier to attract and retain top talent, especially among younger generations who prioritize environmental issues.

Unilever has reported that its strong sustainability

credentials have been a key factor in attracting top graduate talent, with many citing the company's environmental and social commitments as a key reason for wanting to join.

6. Access to Capital and Investor Appeal

As environmental, social, and governance (ESG) factors become increasingly important to investors, companies with strong environmental credentials often enjoy greater access to capital and higher valuations.

As the proverb reminds us, "A good name is more desirable than great riches; to be esteemed is better than silver or gold" (Proverbs 22:1). In business terms, this speaks to the long-term value of building a reputation for environmental responsibility, which can outweigh short-term financial gains.

CHALLENGES TO ENVIRONMENTAL STEWARDSHIP

Despite the clear benefits, maintaining a commitment to environmental stewardship in the modern business environment presents significant challenges:

1. **Short-term Profit Pressures**: The demand for quick returns on investment can discourage the often longer-term investments required for meaningful environmental stewardship.

2. **Complexity of Environmental Issues**: Many environmental challenges are complex and interconnected, making it difficult for companies to fully understand and address their impacts.

3. **Global Supply Chains**: For many companies, a significant portion of their environmental impact occurs in their supply chains, which can be difficult to monitor and influence.

4. **Regulatory Uncertainty**: Changing and sometimes conflicting environmental regulations in different jurisdictions can make it difficult for companies to plan and implement long-term environmental strategies.

5. **Measuring and Valuing Environmental Impact**: Quantifying the full environmental impact of business activities and the value of ecosystem services remains a challenge for many organizations.

6. **Balancing Stakeholder Interests**: Efforts to protect the environment can sometimes conflict with other stakeholder interests, requiring difficult trade-offs.

As the proverb warns, "The greedy stir up conflict, but those who trust in the Lord will prosper" (Proverbs 28:25). This wisdom reminds us of the potential pitfalls of pursuing profit at the expense of environmental responsibility.

STRATEGIES FOR FOSTERING ENVIRONMENTAL STEWARDSHIP

Creating and sustaining a culture of environmental stewardship requires conscious effort and ongoing commitment. Here are key strategies for promoting ethical resource management in business:

1. **Embed Environmental Considerations in Strategy**: Integrate environmental stewardship into core business strategy and decision-making processes at all levels of the organization.

   As the proverb states, "Commit to the Lord whatever you do, and he will establish your plans" (Proverbs 16:3). This underscores the importance of grounding our business strategies in solid ethical and environmental principles.

2. **Set Ambitious Environmental Goals**: Establish clear, measurable environmental goals that drive the organization to continually improve its performance.

3. **Invest in Clean Technologies**: Dedicate resources to developing and implementing cleaner, more efficient technologies across the company.

4. **Foster a Culture of Environmental Responsibility**: Create an organizational culture where all levels value and reward environmental stewardship.

5. **Engage Stakeholders**: Actively engage with employees, customers, suppliers, local communities, and other stakeholders on environmental issues.

6. **Implement Robust Environmental Management Systems**: Develop and maintain comprehensive systems to manage environmental impacts, risks, and opportunities.

7. **Practice Transparency and Accountability**: Be open about environmental challenges and progress and hold the organization accountable for its environmental commitments.

8. **Collaborate for Environmental Solutions**: Partner with other organizations, including competitors where appropriate, to address shared environmental challenges.

9. **Educate and Empower Employees**: Conduct ongoing environmental education and empower employees to contribute to the organization's environmental goals.

10. **Lead by Example**: Leaders must consistently demonstrate a commitment to environmental stewardship in their decisions and actions.

As the proverb advises, "The path of the righteous is like the morning sun, shining ever brighter till the full light of day" (Proverbs 4:18). This wisdom emphasizes the gradual but powerful impact of consistent commitment to ethical practices, including environmental stewardship.

THE PATH FORWARD

As the sun began to set, casting a golden glow over the rainforest canopy, Lucas Alvarez stood on the observation deck and reviewed the new expansion plans Maria had presented. The proposal was bold, innovative, and uncompromising in its commitment to environmental stewardship.

Instead of clearing new land, the plan called for intensifying production on existing plantations through advanced sustainable agricultural techniques. It proposed working with local communities to restore degraded land and create a buffer zone of reforested land around the existing plantation. Most ambitiously, it outlined a long-term strategy to return some of their land to natural forest, enhancing biodiversity and carbon sequestration.

The financial projections were sobering. This path would indeed mean slower growth in the short term. However, as Lucas studied the long-term projections, he saw the potential for a more resilient, sustainable business model that could thrive for generations to come.

"What do you think?" Maria asked, a mixture of hope and determination in her eyes.

Lucas took a deep breath, his eyes sweeping over the vibrant ecosystem that stretched before them. "It won't be easy," he said slowly. "We'll get pushback from some shareholders, and our competitors may see this as an opportunity to undercut us."

He turned to Maria, a newfound determination in his expression. "But it's the right thing to do. Not just for the environment but for the long-term success of our business. We have an opportunity here to set a new standard for our industry and prove that true prosperity and environmental responsibility can go hand in hand.

Maria's face lit up with a broad smile. "I was hoping you'd say that. I've already started putting together a communications plan to get our employees and stakeholders on board.

As they walked back to the main building, Lucas felt a weight lift from his shoulders. The road ahead would be challenging, but in his heart, he knew it was the right one. In a world struggling with climate change, biodiversity loss, and resource depletion, GreenHarvest could become a model of ethical environmental stewardship.

He recalled another proverb: "The plans of the diligent lead to profit as surely as haste leads to poverty" (Proverbs 21:5). By choosing the path of careful, responsible resource management over hasty exploitation, they laid the groundwork for a truly sustainable form of prosperity.

In boardrooms, factories, and offices around the world, similar decisions about environmental stewardship are made every day. As companies grapple with the urgent need to address global environmental challenges while remaining competitive, the wisdom encapsulated in ancient proverbs provides a timeless guide. The scale and complexity of environmental issues may be new, but the principles of responsible stewardship remain constant:

> *"The righteous care for the needs of their animals, but the kindest acts of the wicked are cruel." (Proverbs 12:10).*

> *"A good person leaves an inheritance for their children's children, but a sinner's wealth is stored up for the righteous." (Proverbs 13:22)*

> *"The earth is the Lord's, and everything in it, the world, and all who live in it." (Psalm 24:1)*

These proverbs remind us that in business, as in life, we have a profound responsibility as stewards of the natural world. Our decisions and actions today shape the world we leave to future generations. At a time when environmental crises threaten the very foundations of our economies and societies, the importance of ethical resource management cannot be overstated.

The path of environmental stewardship is rarely the easiest. It requires courage to challenge conventional business models, wisdom to anticipate long-term environmental impacts, and perseverance to pursue sustainable solutions even when they aren't the most profitable in the short term. But as we've seen, it's a path that leads not only to more resilient and sustainable businesses but also to a deeper, more fulfilling way of doing business.

As we continue our exploration of ancient wisdom in modern business, let these principles of environmental stewardship guide us. In the chapters that follow, we will explore related themes- the power of regenerative business models, the importance of intergenerational equity in decision-making, and the role of business in addressing global environmental challenges. Throughout, the lessons learned about the transformative power of ethical resource management will serve as a foundation, a constant reminder of the enduring value of preserving and nurturing the natural world.

Let us move forward, guided by the wisdom of the ages, as we continue to explore the rich intersection of ancient principles and modern business practices. In doing so, we can build organizations that not only thrive financially but also contribute positively to the health of our planet - preserving critical ecosystems, mitigating climate change, and setting a standard of environmental responsibility that elevates the entire business landscape and ensures a thriving world for generations to come.

TWELVE
ETHICAL LEADERSHIP IN CRISIS

"*W*hen *the storm has swept by, the wicked are gone, but the righteous stand firm forever.*" *- Proverbs 10:25*

The gleaming headquarters of Quantum Technologies stood like a beacon against the San Francisco skyline, its glass-and-steel facade reflecting the warm glow of the setting sun. Inside, on the top floor, CEO Alexandra Chen paced her office, her usual composure shattered by the crisis unfolding before her.

Quantum's revolutionary quantum encryption technology, touted as unhackable and deployed by governments and corporations worldwide, had been breached. A sophisticated cyber attack had exposed sensitive data from several high-profile customers. The fallout was immediate and severe. Stock prices plummeted, customers threatened lawsuits, and regulators launched investigations.

As Alexandra stared down at the city below, her mind raced with the magnitude of the challenge. How could they have missed such a critical vulnerability? How many lives and institutions were now at risk because of their oversight? And how could Quantum possibly recover from this devastating blow to its reputation and credibility?

A gentle knock interrupted her thoughts. "Come in," she called, steeling herself for what she knew would be another barrage of bad news.

David Lau, Quantum's Chief Security Officer, entered, his face etched with exhaustion and worry. "Alex, I have the latest report on the breach. It's... not good."

Alexandra nodded and braced herself. "Give it to me straight, David."

"The vulnerability was more fundamental than we first thought. It's not a simple patch job. We're looking at a complete overhaul of the core algorithm. Months of work, at least. And..." he hesitated, clearly struggling with his next words.

"And what, David?" Alexandra pressed.

He met her gaze, his eyes filled with a mixture of guilt and determination. "And there's evidence that some on our team may have known about the vulnerability before the release. They may have downplayed the risks to meet the release deadline."

The revelation hit Alexandra like a physical blow. This wasn't just a technical failure; it was an ethical one. Had they compromised their integrity in their race to be first to market? Had the pressure she was putting on the team to deliver caused them to cut corners?

As the weight of the situation pressed down on her, Alexandra recalled a proverb her grandmother often quoted: "When the storm has swept by, the wicked are gone, but the righteous stand firm forever." The storm was certainly upon them now. The question was: how would Quantum weather it?

Alexandra took a deep breath and straightened her shoulders. "David, I need you to gather the entire executive team. We're going to deal with this head-on, with complete transparency. No cover-ups, no scapegoating. We'll take full responsibility, make it right for our customers, and rebuild our technology from the ground up if we have to."

David's eyes widened in surprise, then filled with relief. "Are you sure, Alex? The short-term consequences..."

"Will be severe," Alexandra finished for him. "But the long-term consequences of trying to hide this or deflect blame would be far worse. We built this company on the promise of trust and safety. It's time we lived up to that promise, even if it hurts."

As David left to gather the team, Alexandra turned back to the window. The sun had set, and the city lights were beginning to twinkle in the gathering darkness. She knew the road ahead would be challenging, but she also knew it was the only way forward. In a world where corporate crises often result in cover-ups and finger-pointing, Quantum had the opportunity to set a new standard for ethical leadership in times of adversity.

Another proverb came to mind: "The integrity of the upright guides them, but the unfaithful are destroyed by their duplicity" (Proverbs 11:3). With renewed determination, Alexandra prepared to lead her company through the storm, guided by the unwavering light of integrity.

THE ESSENCE OF ETHICAL LEADERSHIP IN CRISIS

In the turbulent world of modern business, crises are not a matter of if but when. Ethical leadership in these critical moments goes beyond damage control or public relations. It requires an unwavering commitment to moral principles, transparent communication, and responsible decision-making, even when the stakes are highest.

As another proverb wisely counsels, "The crucible for silver and the furnace for gold, but the Lord tests the heart" (Proverbs 17:3). In a business context, this speaks to how crises reveal the true character of leaders and organizations.

Key aspects of ethical leadership in crisis include:

1. **Transparency**: Be open and honest about the nature and extent of the crisis, even if it's uncomfortable.
2. **Accountability**: Take responsibility for mistakes or oversights instead of looking for scapegoats.
3. **Prioritizing Stakeholder Welfare**: Putting the well-being of affected stakeholders ahead of short-term corporate interests.
4. **Decisive Action**: Make tough decisions quickly, based on ethics rather than expediency.
5. **Empathy:** Demonstrate genuine concern for those affected by the crisis.
6. **Long-term Perspective**: Consider the long-term impact of crisis response, not just immediate damage control.

7. **Ethical Decision-making**: Consistently apply ethical principles to all aspects of crisis management.
8. **Learning and Improvement**: Use the crisis as an opportunity for meaningful organizational change and improvement.

As the proverb states, "The highway of the upright avoids evil; those who guard their ways preserve their lives" (Proverbs 16:17). This serves as a reminder of how ethical leadership can guide organizations safely through crises.

THE BUSINESS CASE FOR ETHICAL LEADERSHIP IN CRISIS

While the moral imperative for ethical leadership in crisis is clear, it's equally important to recognize its tangible business benefits. Organizations that respond to crises with ethical leadership often emerge stronger and more resilient:

1. Trust Restoration and Enhancement

Ethical leadership during a crisis can not only restore trust but can sometimes build it back to pre-crisis levels.

Consider Johnson & Johnson's handling of the 1982 Tylenol crisis, which we've discussed in earlier chapters. The company's swift, transparent, and consumer-focused response not only saved the brand but also enhanced J&J's reputation for corporate responsibility.

2. Organizational Learning and Improvement

Crises handled ethically often become catalysts for meaningful organizational change and improvement.

Starbucks' response to a racial bias incident in 2018, which included closing stores for company-wide racial bias training, demonstrated how ethical leadership can turn a crisis into an opportunity for significant organizational improvement.

3. Employee Loyalty and Engagement

Ethical leadership in times of crisis can strengthen employee loyalty and engagement, which are critical factors in recovery and long-term success.

Marriott International's response to the COVID-19 pandemic, which prioritized employee well-being even at a significant cost to the company, has been credited with maintaining strong employee loyalty and positioning the company for a stronger recovery.

4. Stakeholder Relationships

Ethical crisis leadership can strengthen relationships with various stakeholders, from customers to regulators.

Microsoft's handling of the 2017 WannaCry ransomware attack, which included releasing security patches even for outdated systems that were no longer supported, demonstrated a commitment to the public good that enhanced its reputation with customers and regulators alike.

5. Long-term Resilience

Organizations that respond to crises ethically often develop greater long-term resilience and adaptability.

Patagonia's consistent ethical responses to challenges ranging from supply chain issues to environmental concerns have contributed to its reputation for resilience and adaptability in the face of change.

6. Competitive Differentiation

Ethical leadership can serve as a powerful differentiator in industries where unethical responses to crises are common.

As the proverb reminds us, "Like a muddied spring or a polluted well are the righteous who give way to the wicked" (Proverbs 25:26). In business terms, this speaks to how maintaining ethical standards, especially during crises, can distinguish a company in a marketplace where such standards are often compromised.

CHALLENGES TO ETHICAL LEADERSHIP IN CRISIS

Despite the clear benefits, maintaining ethical leadership during a crisis presents significant challenges:

1. **Pressure for Quick Fixes**: The urgency of a crisis can create pressure for quick fixes that may compromise ethical standards.

2. **Incomplete Information**: Crises often unfold in an environment of uncertainty, where leaders must make decisions without complete information.

3. **Stakeholder Pressure**: Different stakeholders may push for responses that conflict with ethical principles or with each other.

4. **Short-term Financial Impact**: Ethical responses to crises may involve short-term financial costs, creating tension with financial stakeholders.

5. **Legal and Regulatory Complexity**: The legal and regulatory landscape during a crisis can be complex, sometimes seeming to incentivize less than fully transparent responses.

6. **Emotional Stress**: The high-stakes, high-stress nature of crises can cloud judgment and make ethical decisions more difficult.

As the proverb warns, "Whoever walks in integrity walks securely, but whoever takes crooked paths will be found out" (Proverbs 10:9). This wisdom reminds us of the long-term risks of compromising ethical standards, even when the short-term pressures of a crisis seem to encourage it.

STRATEGIES FOR FOSTERING ETHICAL LEADERSHIP IN CRISIS

Developing the capacity for ethical crisis leadership requires deliberate effort and ongoing commitment. Here are key strategies for fostering ethical crisis leadership:

1. **Develop a Strong Ethical Foundation**: Cultivate a robust ethical culture and clear values to guide decision-making in times of crisis.

   As the proverb says, "When the storm has swept by, the wicked are gone, but the righteous stand firm forever" (Proverbs 10:25). This underscores the importance of building a strong ethical foundation that can withstand the storms of crisis.

2. **Create a Crisis Response Plan**: Develop comprehensive crisis response plans that explicitly address ethical considerations.

3. **Practice Transparent Communication**: Foster a culture of open, honest communication that can be maintained under the pressure of a crisis.

4. **Empower Ethical Decision-Making**: Provide training and frameworks that empower leaders at all levels to make ethical decisions in high-pressure situations.

5. **Prioritize Stakeholder Welfare**: Incorporate a stakeholder-centered approach into crisis response strategies, prioritizing the well-being of those affected by the crisis.

6. **Cultivate Emotional Intelligence**: Develop leaders' emotional intelligence to help them manage the stress and complexity of crises while maintaining ethical standards.

7. **Learn from Past Crises**: Systematically review and learn from past crises within the organization and in other companies and industries.

8. **Build a Culture of Accountability**: Foster a culture where individuals and the organization as a whole take responsibility for mistakes and learn from them.

9. **Engage in Scenario Planning**: Conduct regular ethical crisis scenario planning to prepare leaders for difficult decisions.

10. **Lead by Example**: Top leaders must consistently demonstrate ethical behavior, especially in times of crisis.

As the proverb advises, "The wise in heart accept commands, but a chattering fool comes to ruin" (Proverbs 10:8). This wisdom emphasizes the importance of leaders who can listen, learn, and apply ethical principles in the heat of a crisis.

THE PATH FORWARD

As the first rays of dawn broke over the San Francisco skyline, Alexandra Chen stood before her assembled executive team, board members, and key stakeholders. The room buzzed with excitement, all eyes on her as she prepared to outline Quantum's response to the crisis.

Taking a deep breath, Alexandra began. "Ladies and gentlemen, we are at a critical juncture. Our technology, which we promised was unhackable, has been breached. The trust of our customers and the public has been shaken. We have a choice.

We can try to minimize this breach, deflect blame, or hide behind legal maneuvers. Or we can face this crisis head-on, with complete transparency and a commitment to make things right, no matter the cost."

She paused, meeting the gaze of every person in the room. "I choose the latter. We will take full responsibility for this breach. We will be completely transparent about what happened, how it happened, and what we're doing to fix it. We will compensate affected customers and work tirelessly to rebuild our technology from the ground up with even stronger security measures.

A murmur went through the room. Alexandra saw a mix of reactions - concern, skepticism, but also respect and relief.

"I know this path will be difficult," she continued. "Our stock will take a hit. We may face legal challenges. Our reputation will suffer in the short term. But by adhering to our values of integrity and transparency, we have the opportunity to emerge from this crisis stronger, more trusted, and better equipped to fulfill our mission of providing true security in the digital age."

As she outlined the detailed crisis response plan, Alexandra felt a sense of clarity and purpose she hadn't experienced since the crisis began. The road ahead would be challenging, but she knew in her heart it was the right one.

In the weeks and months that followed, Quantum weathered a storm of media scrutiny, regulatory investigations, and market volatility. But out of the chaos, something unexpected began to emerge. Customers praised the company's honesty and commitment to making things right. Employees rallied around the mission to rebuild their technology on a stronger ethical foundation. Even some investors expressed confidence in the company's long-term prospects after the initial shock, impressed by the integrity of her leadership in the face of the crisis.

A year later, Alexandra stood in front of her team again, this time with a very different story to tell. "I'm proud to announce that our new quantum encryption technology has passed the industry's most rigorous independent security audits. Not only have we fixed the vulnerabilities that led to the breach, but we've set a new standard for transparency and security in our field."

She paused and looked around at her team's faces, seeing the pride and determination reflected in them. "But more importantly, we've proven that ethical leadership can guide a company through even the worst storms. We chose integrity over expediency, transparency over obfuscation, and long-term trust over short-term damage control. And we are stronger for it.

As the meeting adjourned, Alexandra felt a profound sense of accomplishment. In a world where corporate crises often lead to cover-ups and ethical compromises, Quantum had chosen a different path - and emerged not only intact but renewed.

In boardrooms and crisis centers worldwide, similar choices about ethical leadership are made every day. As companies grapple with crises in an increasingly complex and interconnected global economy, the wisdom encapsulated in ancient proverbs provides a timeless guide. The nature of crises may change, but the principles of ethical leadership remain constant:

> *"When the storm has swept by, the wicked are gone, but the righteous stand firm forever." (Proverbs 10:25).*

"The integrity of the upright guides them, but the unfaithful are destroyed by their duplicity." (Proverbs 11:3).

"Whoever walks in integrity walks securely, but whoever takes crooked paths will be found out." (Proverbs 10:9)

These proverbs remind us that in business, as in life, our true character is revealed in times of crisis. How we respond to challenges, how we treat those affected by our mistakes, and how we rebuild after failure - these actions define us far more than our successes in times of plenty.

The path of ethical leadership in a crisis is rarely the easiest. It requires courage to face hard truths, wisdom to make tough decisions, and perseverance to rebuild on a foundation of integrity. But as we've seen, it's a path that leads not only to recovery but often to renewal and unprecedented growth.

As we conclude our exploration of ancient wisdom in modern business, let these principles of ethical crisis leadership be our guiding light. They remind us that true business success is measured not just in profits or market share but in the trust we build, the lives we touch, and the legacy we leave.

Let us move forward, guided by the wisdom of the ages, as we navigate the complex challenges of the modern business world. In doing so, we can build organizations that not only withstand the storms of crisis but emerge stronger, more ethical, and better equipped to positively impact the world. After all, it is not the absence of crises that defines great companies but how they face them with integrity, compassion, and an unwavering commitment to doing the right thing.

CONCLUSION: THE TIMELESS WISDOM OF ETHICAL BUSINESS

"The fear of the Lord is the beginning of wisdom, and knowledge of the Holy One is understanding." - Proverbs 9:10

The sun dipped below the horizon, painting the sky with shades of orange and purple as Dr. Elizabeth Morgan took the podium. A sea of eager faces filled the auditorium before her - students, faculty, and business leaders gathered for Stanford University's annual Ethics in Business Symposium.

Elizabeth, a renowned business ethicist and author, took a deep breath, her fingers brushing the worn leather cover of her grandmother's Book of Proverbs. This book had been her constant companion throughout her career, a source of wisdom and guidance as she navigated the complex world of modern business ethics.

"Ladies and gentlemen," she began, her voice clear and steady, "we stand at a crossroads in the world of business. In an era of rapid technological advancement, global interconnectedness, and unprecedented challenges, the pursuit of profit often seems at odds with ethical behavior."

She paused, her gaze sweeping the audience. "But I'm here to argue that this perceived conflict is not only false, it's dangerous. The wisdom of the ages, encapsulated in ancient proverbs, offers us a roadmap for conducting business with integrity, purpose, and long-term success."

As Elizabeth began her speech, she reflected on the journey that brought her to this moment. From her early days as a junior executive grappling with ethical dilemmas to her tenure as a corporate ethics officer to her current role as an educator and thought leader, she has seen firsthand the power of applying timeless wisdom to modern business challenges.

"Throughout this book," she continued, "we have explored how the principles embedded in ancient proverbs can guide us in addressing the most pressing issues in business ethics today. Let us revisit these lessons and consider how they can shape the future of ethical business practice.

THE FOUNDATION OF INTEGRITY

"We began our journey by examining the fundamental role of integrity in business," Elizabeth said, her voice growing passionate. "As Proverbs 11:3 reminds us, 'The integrity of the upright guides them, but the unfaithful are destroyed by their duplicity.'"

She told the story of Sarah Smith, the CEO, who chose to delay a product launch rather than compromise user privacy. "This decision," Elizabeth emphasized, "illustrates how integrity can guide leaders through complex ethical dilemmas. It's not about following a set of rules; it's about cultivating a deep commitment to doing the right thing, even when it's difficult."

The audience nodded in agreement, many furiously scribbling notes.

"In a world where corporate scandals regularly make headlines, companies built on a foundation of integrity stand out. They earn the trust of customers, the loyalty of employees, and the respect of communities. This trust becomes an invaluable asset, far more valuable than any short-term gain achieved through ethical compromise.

FAIR DEALING: THE CORNERSTONE OF SUSTAINABLE BUSINESS

Elizabeth moved on to the next topic. "We then explored the principle of fair dealing, guided by the wisdom of Proverbs 16:11: 'Honest scales and balances belong to the Lord; all the weights in the bag are of his making.'"

She recalled the story of Mark Thompson, the CEO who, faced with rising costs, chose to innovate rather than exploit his suppliers. "This example," she noted, "illustrates how fair dealing can drive innovation and build stronger, more resilient business relationships."

"In our globalized economy, where supply chains span continents and stakeholders are diverse, the principle of fair dealing is more important than ever. It's not just about following the letter of the law but about fostering a spirit of fairness and mutual benefit in all our business interactions.

THE PERILS OF GREED

Elizabeth's tone grew somber as she moved on to the next topic. "We also confronted the destructive power of greed, heeding the warning of Proverbs 15:27.: 'The greedy bring ruin to their households, but the one who hates bribes will live.'"

She told the cautionary tale of Emma Reeves, the pharmaceutical executive who initially put profits ahead of patient safety, only to later choose the path of ethical responsibility.

"The pursuit of profit is not inherently unethical," Elizabeth clarified. "But when it becomes all-consuming, when it blinds us to the consequences of our actions, it can have devastating results. We've seen how companies driven by unchecked greed often end up destroying value rather than creating it."

The audience shifted uncomfortably, many recognizing the truth in her words.

"The antidote to greed," she continued, "is not to abandon the pursuit of profit but to take a broader, more holistic view of what constitutes success in business. It's about creating value for all stakeholders, not just shareholders. It's about thinking in terms of generations, not just quarters.

WISE LEADERSHIP: THE POWER OF ETHICAL DECISION-MAKING

Elizabeth's eyes sparkled as she moved on to the next topic. "We looked at the critical role of wise leadership, guided by Proverbs 15:22: 'Plans fail for lack of counsel, but with many advisers they succeed.'"

She told the story of Michael Rodriguez, the CEO who decided to delay a product launch to address potential environmental impacts despite short-term financial pressures.

"Wise leadership," Elizabeth emphasized, "is not about having all the answers. It's about asking the right questions, seeking diverse perspectives, and having the courage to make difficult decisions based on ethical principles rather than expediency."

She paused, letting the weight of her words sink in. "In an era of rapid change and increasing complexity, wise leadership is more important than ever. It's the compass that guides organizations through uncertainty, balancing short-term pressures with long-term sustainability.

BUILDING A GOOD NAME: THE VALUE OF ETHICAL REPUTATION

"We then explored the immense value of an ethical reputation," Elizabeth continued. "As Proverbs 22:1 tells us, 'A good name is more desirable than great riches; to be esteemed is better than silver or gold.'"

She told the story of Olivia Hartley, the ethics officer who led her company through a reputational crisis by championing transparency and accountability.

"In our hyper-connected world, where information travels at the speed of light, a company's reputation is its most valuable asset. Building and maintaining an ethical reputation requires constant vigilance and a genuine commitment to living up to one's stated values."

Elizabeth's voice grew passionate. "It's not about creating the perfect public image; it's about consistently doing the right thing, even when no one is watching. Companies with strong ethical reputations weather crises better and enjoy greater customer loyalty, employee engagement, and stakeholder trust."

ETHICAL EMPLOYEE RELATIONS: TREATING WORKERS JUSTLY

Elizabeth's tone softened as she moved on to the next topic. "We also examined the critical importance of ethical employee relations, guided by Proverbs 22:16: 'One who oppresses the poor to increase his wealth and one who gives gifts to the rich —both come to poverty.'"

She told the story of Amanda Chen, the CEO, who chose to improve the working conditions and treatment of her employees, even at the expense of short-term profits.

"At a time when talent is often a company's most valuable resource, treating employees fairly is not just an ethical imperative - it's a business necessity," Elizabeth explained. "Companies that prioritize fair compensation, safe working conditions, and opportunities for growth and development are not only doing the right thing by their employees, they are creating more productive, innovative, and resilient organizations."

The audience nodded in agreement, many thinking of their own workplace experiences.

"Ethical employee relations goes beyond compliance with labor laws," she continued. "It's about recognizing the inherent dignity and value of every worker, from the C-suite to the shop floor. It's about creating workplaces where people can thrive, contribute their best, and find meaning in their work."

THE WISDOM OF LONG-TERM THINKING

Elizabeth's voice took on a thoughtful tone as she moved to the next principle. "We explored the wisdom of long-term thinking, inspired by Proverbs 21:5: 'The plans of the diligent lead to profit as surely as haste leads to poverty.'"

She told the story of Daniel Hawthorne, the technology CEO who decided to delay a product launch to address ethical concerns, ultimately resulting in a stronger, more sustainable business model.

"In a business world that is often driven by quarterly results and short-term thinking, the wisdom of taking a long-term view cannot be overstated," Elizabeth emphasized. "It's about looking beyond immediate gains to consider the broader, long-term implications of our decisions."

She paused, letting the idea sink in. "Companies that think long term are better positioned to manage uncertainty, invest in innovation, and create lasting value. They're more likely to consider the environmental and social impacts of their actions, leading to more sustainable and responsible business practices."

ETHICAL COMMUNICATION: TRUTH TELLING IN BUSINESS

Elizabeth's tone grew serious as she moved on to the next topic. "We delved into the critical importance of ethical communication, guided by Proverbs 12:22.: 'The Lord detests lying lips, but he delights in people who are trustworthy.'"

She shared the story of Rachel Thompson, the communications executive who chose transparency in the face of a product safety issue, ultimately strengthening her company's reputation and stakeholder relationships.

"In an age of information overload and 'fake news,' ethical communication in business is more important than ever," Elizabeth said. "It's not just about avoiding lies; it's about proactively sharing the truth, even when it's uncomfortable or potentially damaging in the short term."

The audience leaned in, many recognizing the challenges of maintaining transparency in their own organizations.

"Ethical communication builds trust, promotes better decision-making, and creates a culture of openness and integrity," she continued. "It is the foundation for strong relationships with all stakeholders, from employees to customers to investors."

ETHICAL INNOVATION: CREATING VALUE RESPONSIBLY

Elizabeth's eyes lit up as she moved on to the next principle. "We explored the concept of ethical innovation, inspired by Proverbs 24:3-4.: 'By wisdom, a house is built, and through understanding, it is established; through knowledge, its rooms are filled with rare and beautiful treasures.'"

She told the story of Dr. Samantha Patel, the researcher who decided to shift her team's focus to developing a more ethical and sustainable technology, even at the cost of short-term market advantage.

"Innovation is the lifeblood of economic growth and progress," Elizabeth emphasized. "But in our pursuit of the new and the groundbreaking, we must never lose sight of our ethical responsibilities. Ethical innovation is about creating value in a way that benefits society, respects human rights, and preserves our environment."

She paused, her eyes sweeping the audience. "It's not just about asking, 'Can we do this?' but 'Should we do this?' and 'How can we do this responsibly? Companies that embrace ethical innovation avoid potential pitfalls and often uncover new opportunities to create meaningful, sustainable value."

ETHICAL CONFLICT RESOLUTION: WISDOM IN DISPUTES

Elizabeth's tone grew thoughtful as she moved on to the next topic. "We examined the principle of ethical conflict resolution, guided by Proverbs 17:14: 'Starting a quarrel is like breaching a dam; so drop the matter before a dispute breaks out.'"

She told the story of Amelia Wu, the ethics officer who guided her company through a complex international dispute by focusing on underlying interests and ethical principles rather than entrenched positions.

"In business, as in life, conflict is inevitable," said Elizabeth. "But how we handle those conflicts can make all the difference. Ethical conflict resolution is not about avoiding disagreement, but about managing it in a way that upholds moral principles, preserves relationships, and ultimately strengthens the organization."

The audience nodded, many recognizing the challenges of managing conflict in their own professional lives.

"By approaching conflict with wisdom, patience, and a commitment to ethical principles, we can turn potential crises into opportunities for growth, innovation, and stronger stakeholder relationships," she continued.

ENVIRONMENTAL STEWARDSHIP: ETHICAL RESOURCE MANAGEMENT

Elizabeth's voice took on a note of urgency as she moved on to the next principle. "We explored the critical importance of environmental stewardship, inspired by Proverbs 12:10: 'The righteous care for the needs of their animals, but the kindest acts of the wicked are cruel.'"

She told the story of Lucas Alvarez, the CEO who chose to prioritize conservation and reforestation in his company's expansion plans, setting a new standard for ethical resource management in his industry.

"In an era of climate change, biodiversity loss, and resource depletion, environmental stewardship is not just an ethical imperative - it's a business necessity," Elizabeth explained. "It's about recognizing that our businesses are part of, and dependent on, the natural world."

She paused, her gaze intense. "Companies that embrace environmental stewardship not only mitigate risk and ensure long-term sustainability, they often uncover new opportunities for innovation and value creation. They recognize that true prosperity cannot come at the expense of the planet we all call home.

ETHICAL LEADERSHIP IN CRISIS

Elizabeth's tone grew solemn as she addressed the final theme. "We concluded our exploration with a look at ethical leadership in crisis, guided by Proverbs 10:25: 'When the storm has swept by, the wicked are gone, but the righteous stand firm forever.'"

She shared the story of Alexandra Chen, the tech CEO who chose transparency and accountability in the face of a major security breach, ultimately strengthening her company's culture and stakeholder relationships.

"Crises test the mettle of leaders and organizations like nothing else," Elizabeth pointed out. "It is in these moments of truth that our commitment to ethical principles is truly tested. Ethical leadership in a crisis is about maintaining integrity under pressure, putting the welfare of stakeholders ahead of short-term interests, and seeing crises as opportunities for meaningful change and improvement."

The audience sat in rapt attention, many thinking of crises they had faced in their own careers.

"Leaders who navigate crises with ethical courage not only guide their organizations through the immediate challenges but often emerge stronger, with increased trust and resilience," she continued.

THE PATH FORWARD: INTEGRATING ANCIENT WISDOM IN MODERN BUSINESS

As Elizabeth neared the end of her speech, her voice took on a tone of both challenge and inspiration. "Throughout this book, we've seen how the wisdom encapsulated in ancient proverbs can light our way through the complex ethical challenges of modern business. But knowledge without action is useless. The question now is: How will we integrate these timeless principles into our daily business practices?

She paused, her eyes sweeping the room. "I challenge each of you to become an ambassador for ethical business. Whether you're a CEO, a middle manager, an entrepreneur, or a student preparing to enter the business world, you have the power to make a difference."

Elizabeth's voice grew passionate. "Imagine a business world where integrity is the norm, not the exception, where long-term value creation trumps short-term profit-seeking. Where people are treated with dignity, the environment is respected, and innovation is driven by a desire to solve real-world problems, not just maximize profits."

She smiled, her eyes sparkling with conviction. "This vision is not some naive utopia. As we've seen through the stories and principles we've explored, it's a practical, achievable reality. Companies that embrace ethical business practices not only do good, they often do better in the long run.

Elizabeth's tone became reflective. "The ethical business journey is not always easy. It takes courage to stand up for what's right, wisdom to navigate complex dilemmas, and perseverance to stay the course in the face of short-term pressures. But it's a journey worth taking, not just for the success it can bring to our organizations but for the positive impact we can have on the world.

She closed her grandmother's book of Proverbs, holding it close to her heart. "As we conclude, let us remember the words of Proverbs 9:10: 'The fear of the Lord is the beginning of wisdom, and knowledge of the Holy One is understanding.' In a business context, this reminds us that true wisdom in business starts with a deep respect for ethical principles and a recognition of our responsibility to something greater than ourselves."

Elizabeth's voice rose with conviction for her final words. "Let us go out and build businesses that not only make a profit but also add value to society, respect our planet, and uplift the human spirit. In doing so, we will find not only success but also fulfillment, knowing that our work contributes to a better world for generations to come."

As applause filled the room, Elizabeth felt a sense of accomplishment and anticipation. The journey of exploring ancient wisdom in modern business had been enlightening, but she knew it was only the beginning. The real work lay ahead in the daily decisions and actions of business leaders around the world.

She stepped down from the podium, ready to engage with the audience, to hear their stories, their challenges, and their aspirations for ethical business. For Elizabeth knew that the true power of wisdom lies not in its preaching, but in its application. And in the complex, fast-paced world of modern business, the timeless wisdom of proverbs could light the way to a more ethical, sustainable, and prosperous future.

As business leaders, employees, and students filed out of the auditorium, the buzz of lively discussion filled the air. Elizabeth's words had struck a chord, igniting a spark of inspiration and reflection in each person. Far from being outdated or irrelevant, the ancient wisdom she shared proved to be a powerful lens through which to view the challenges and opportunities of modern business.

In the days, weeks, and months that followed, the impact of Elizabeth's speech and the book it summarized rippled through the business world. CEOs re-evaluated their leadership styles and incorporated ethical considerations more deeply into their decision-making processes. Entrepreneurs began to build their start-ups on a foundation of integrity and long-term thinking. Business schools incorporated the study of proverbs and ethical wisdom into their curricula, recognizing the need to cultivate not just skilled but wise business leaders.

However, perhaps the most profound changes occurred in the daily interactions and decisions of countless individuals in the business world. A manager, remembering the adage about the value of a good name, chose transparency over obfuscation in addressing a product defect. An employee, inspired by the teachings of ethical conflict resolution, found the courage to speak up about a workplace issue, leading to positive changes in company culture. A board member, reflecting on the warnings against greed, advocated for more sustainable, stakeholder-friendly policies.

These individual actions, seemingly small in isolation, began to coalesce into a larger movement. Companies known for their ethical practices began to outperform their peers, attracting top talent, loyal customers, and socially conscious investors. The business narrative began to shift, with success stories increasingly highlighting not just financial performance but ethical leadership and positive societal impact.

Of course, challenges remained. The pressures of short-term thinking, the allure of easy profits, and the complexities of global business continued to test the resolve of even the most ethically-minded leaders. But armed with the timeless wisdom of proverbs, more and more businesses found the strength and guidance to navigate these challenges with integrity.

As the years passed, Elizabeth continued her work, speaking, writing, and advising, always with her grandmother's book of Proverbs close at hand. She watched with pride and hope as a new generation of business leaders emerged, one that saw ethical behavior not as a constraint on success, but as the very foundation of it.

In boardrooms and offices, in startups and multinational corporations, the ancient wisdom of proverbs became a living, breathing part of business culture. The words that had guided generations through the complexities of life proved equally adept at illuminating the path through the intricacies of modern commerce.

And so, the journey that began with a simple book of Proverbs continued an ever-evolving exploration of how ancient wisdom could create not just profitable businesses but a better world. In the end, the true measure of business success lay not just in the profits generated but in the lives improved, the communities strengthened, and the legacy left for future generations.

As the sun set on another day in the world of business, countless leaders, guided by the wisdom of the ages, made decisions that would shape the future. In each of these moments, big and small, the power of proverbs for profit—ethical, sustainable, meaningful profit—continued to prove its enduring value.

The story of business ethics, like the proverbs themselves, had no true ending. It was a continuous journey of learning, growth, and striving to do better. But with each step guided by timeless wisdom, the path forward became clearer, the destination more inspiring, and the journey itself more fulfilling.

And so, as we close this book, we do not end our exploration of ethics in business. Rather, we begin anew, armed with ancient insights and modern understanding, ready to face the challenges and opportunities that lie ahead. For in the ever-changing world of business, the wisdom of proverbs remains a constant guide, a beacon of integrity lighting the way toward a more ethical, prosperous, and sustainable future.

APPENDIX A: THE ETHICAL DECISION-MAKING FRAMEWORK

In the complex world of modern business, leaders often face situations where the right course of action isn't immediately clear. This framework, based on the timeless wisdom we've explored throughout this book, provides a step-by-step guide to navigating ethical dilemmas. By following these steps, you'll approach decisions with greater clarity, consistency, and ethical grounding.

STEP 1: IDENTIFY THE ETHICAL ISSUE

Begin by clearly articulating the ethical dilemma you face. What decision must you make? What principles or values are at stake?

Consider the proverb: "The simple believe anything, but the prudent give thought to their steps" (Proverbs 14:15).

Ask yourself:

- What are the facts of the situation?

- Who are the stakeholders affected by the decision?
- What ethical principles are involved (e.g., honesty, fairness, respect for persons, environmental stewardship)?

STEP 2: GATHER RELEVANT INFORMATION

Make sure you have all the information you need to make an informed decision. Seek out different perspectives and consider the broader context.

Recall the wisdom: "Plans fail for lack of counsel, but with many advisers, they succeed" (Proverbs 15:22).

Key actions:

- Consult with peers, experts, or mentors
- Research relevant laws, regulations, and industry standards
- Consider historical precedents or similar situations in your industry

STEP 3: CONSIDER ALTERNATIVE ACTIONS

Brainstorm various possible courses of action. Don't limit yourself to obvious solutions; think creatively about different approaches.

Remember: "The path of life leads upward for the prudent to keep them from going down to the realm of the dead" (Proverbs 15:24).

For each alternative, ask:

- What are the potential short- and long-term consequences?
- How does this option align with our company's values and ethical standards?
- What would happen if this decision became public?

STEP 4: EVALUATE THE OPTIONS

Evaluate each alternative against ethical principles and potential outcomes. Consider both the intent and the consequences of each action.

Reflect on the proverb: "The integrity of the upright guides them, but the unfaithful are destroyed by their duplicity" (Proverbs 11:3).

Evaluation criteria:

- Which option best upholds ethical principles?
- What are the potential risks and rewards of each option?
- How would this decision impact our stakeholders?
- Is this option consistent with our long-term goals and values?

STEP 5: MAKE THE DECISION

Choose the course of action that best aligns with ethical principles and creates the most positive outcome for all stakeholders.

Consider the wisdom: "Commit to the Lord whatever you do, and he will establish your plans" (Proverbs 16:3).

Key considerations:

- Can you clearly articulate the ethical reasoning behind your decision?
- Would you be comfortable with this decision being reported in the media?
- Does this decision reflect the kind of company you want to be?

STEP 6: IMPLEMENT THE DECISION

Follow through on your chosen course of action. Be clear in your communication and transparent in your reasoning.

Remember: "The tongue of the righteous is choice silver, but the heart of the wicked is of little value" (Proverbs 10:20).

Implementation steps:

- Clearly communicate the decision and its rationale to all stakeholders
- Develop an action plan with specific steps and timelines
- Assign ownership and ensure accountability

STEP 7: REFLECT AND LEARN

After implementing your decision, take time to reflect on the outcome and learn from the experience.

Heed the proverb: "The way of fools seems right to them, but the wise listen to advice" (Proverbs 12:15).

Reflection questions:

- What were the actual results of the decision?
- Did the decision meet our ethical standards?

- What did we learn from the process?
- How can we apply these lessons to future decisions?

By consistently applying this framework, you'll develop a habit of ethical decision-making that will guide you through even the most complex business challenges. Remember, ethical leadership isn't about having all the answers; it's about approaching every decision with integrity, wisdom, and a commitment to doing the right thing.

As you use this framework, keep in mind the overarching principle we've explored throughout this book: true business success comes not from short-term gains or clever maneuvering but from consistently making decisions that create value, uphold integrity, and contribute positively to all stakeholders.

In the words of the ancient proverb, "The blessing of the Lord brings wealth, without painful toil for it" (Proverbs 10:22). By grounding our business decisions in ethical principles, we pave the way for sustainable success and a legacy of positive impact.

APPENDIX B: PROVERBS FOR QUICK ETHICAL GUIDANCE

In the fast-paced world of business, leaders often need quick wisdom to guide their decisions. This collection of proverbs, organized by common business themes, offers readily accessible ethical guidance. Use these ancient insights to light your way through today's business challenges.

LEADERSHIP AND DECISION MAKING

1. "Where there is no vision, the people perish." - Proverbs 29:18 *Application*: Set clear, ethical goals for your organization.
2. "Plans fail for lack of counsel, but with many advisers they succeed." - Proverbs 15:22 *Application*: Seek diverse perspectives before making important decisions.
3. "The way of fools seems right to them, but the wise listen to advice." - Proverbs 12:15 *Application*: Remain open to feedback and continuous learning.

4. "A wise king winnows out the wicked; he drives the threshing wheel over them." - Proverbs 20:26 *Application*: Address unethical behavior promptly and decisively.

INTEGRITY AND TRUST

1. "The integrity of the upright guides them, but the unfaithful are destroyed by their duplicity." - Proverbs 11:3 *Application*: Let integrity guide all business decisions and actions.
2. "Whoever walks in integrity walks securely, but whoever takes crooked paths will be found out." - Proverbs 10:9 *Application*: Build trust through consistent ethical behavior.
3. "The Lord detests lying lips, but he delights in people who are trustworthy." - Proverbs 12:22 *Application*: Prioritize honesty in all communications.
4. "To do what is right and just is more acceptable to the Lord than sacrifice." - Proverbs 21:3 *Application*: Prioritize ethical actions over mere appearances or token gestures.

FINANCIAL MANAGEMENT AND FAIR DEALING

1. "Dishonest money dwindles away, but whoever gathers money little by little makes it grow." - Proverbs 13:11 *Application*: Build sustainable wealth through ethical practices.
2. "The rich rule over the poor, and the borrower is slave to the lender." - Proverbs 22:7 *Application*: Manage

debt responsibly and consider the ethical implications of financial power dynamics.

3. "Honest scales and balances belong to the Lord; all the weights in the bag are of his making." - Proverbs 16:11 *Application*: Ensure fair and transparent financial practices.

4. "Better a little with righteousness than much gain with injustice." - Proverbs 16:8 *Application*: Prioritize ethical practices over short-term financial gains.

EMPLOYEE RELATIONS

1. "Those who oppress the poor to increase their wealth and those who give gifts to the rich—both come to poverty." - Proverbs 22:16 *Application*: Treat all employees fairly, regardless of their status.

2. "A generous person will prosper; whoever refreshes others will be refreshed." - Proverbs 11:25 *Application*: Invest in employee well-being and development.

3. "One who is slack in his work is brother to one who destroys." - Proverbs 18:9 *Application*: Encourage diligence and quality work.

4. "Servants cannot be corrected by mere words; though they understand, they will not respond." - Proverbs 29:19 *Application*: Lead by example and provide clear expectations and consequences.

CUSTOMER RELATIONS AND MARKETING

1. "The tongue has the power of life and death, and those who love it will eat its fruit." - Proverbs 18:21

Application: Use honest, responsible marketing practices.

2. "A good name is more desirable than great riches; to be esteemed is better than silver or gold." - Proverbs 22:1 *Application*: Prioritize building a strong, ethical reputation.

3. "Do not exploit the poor because they are poor and do not crush the needy in court." - Proverbs 22:22 *Application*: Treat all customers fairly, regardless of their economic status.

4. "A gossip betrays a confidence, but a trustworthy person keeps a secret." - Proverbs 11:13 *Application*: Respect customer privacy and confidentiality.

INNOVATION AND LONG-TERM THINKING

1. "The plans of the diligent lead to profit as surely as haste leads to poverty." - Proverbs 21:5 *Application*: Invest in careful planning and sustainable innovation.

2. "The wise store up choice food and olive oil, but fools gulp theirs down." - Proverbs 21:20 *Application*: Balance current needs with future sustainability.

3. "The prudent see danger and take refuge, but the simple keep going and pay the penalty." - Proverbs 22:3 *Application*: Anticipate and prepare for potential ethical challenges.

4. "By wisdom a house is built, and through understanding it is established." - Proverbs 24:3 *Application*: Build your business on a foundation of ethical wisdom.

ENVIRONMENTAL STEWARDSHIP

1. "The righteous care for the needs of their animals, but the kindest acts of the wicked are cruel." - Proverbs 12:10 *Application*: Extend ethical consideration to environmental impacts.
2. "A prudent person foresees danger and takes precautions. The simpleton goes blindly on and suffers the consequences." - Proverbs 27:12 (NLT) *Application*: Anticipate and mitigate environmental risks.
3. "The earth is the Lord's, and everything in it, the world, and all who live in it." - Psalm 24:1 *Application*: Recognize the broader context and responsibility of business operations.

CONFLICT RESOLUTION

1. "Starting a quarrel is like breaching a dam; so drop the matter before a dispute breaks out." - Proverbs 17:14 *Application*: Address conflicts early and constructively.
2. "A gentle answer turns away wrath, but a harsh word stirs up anger." - Proverbs 15:1 *Application*: Use respectful communication to de-escalate conflicts.
3. "The first to present his case seems right, till another comes forward and questions him." - Proverbs 18:17 *Application*: Consider all perspectives in a dispute before making judgments.

CRISIS MANAGEMENT

1. "When the storm has swept by, the wicked are gone, but the righteous stand firm forever." - Proverbs 10:25 *Application*: Maintain ethical standards even in times of crisis.
2. "The prudent see danger and take refuge, but the simple keep going and pay the penalty." - Proverbs 27:12 *Application*: Anticipate potential crises and prepare ethical response plans.
3. "Whoever conceals their sins does not prosper, but the one who confesses and renounces them finds mercy." - Proverbs 28:13 *Application*: Address mistakes openly and take responsibility for correcting them.

As you navigate the complex terrain of modern business, let these sayings serve as your ethical compass. Remember that true business success comes not from clever maneuvering or short-term gain but from consistently making decisions that create value, uphold integrity, and contribute positively to all stakeholders.

In the words of the ancient proverb, "Commit to the Lord whatever you do, and he will establish your plans" (Proverbs 16:3). By grounding our business practices in timeless ethical principles, we pave the way for sustainable success and a legacy of positive impact.

ABOUT THE AUTHOR

Richard French stands at the intersection of technological innovation and ethical leadership. One of the country's foremost authorities on Robotic Process Automation and AI, French has been a driving force behind several companies that have reshaped the business landscape. His career, which includes executive roles at Oracle and Nokia and CEO positions at several successful startups, has been defined by a commitment to ethical decision-making in rapid technological change.

French's expertise spans various technologies, from software and mobile applications to AI and automation. He has led organizations on five continents, navigating the complex ethical terrain of global business expansion. Throughout his career, French has demonstrated that ethical leadership and business success are not mutually exclusive. His philosophy that "people work with us, not for us" has been instrumental in building ethical, high-performing teams in diverse cultural contexts.

Trained as a mathematician, French brings an analytical mind to the often ambiguous world of business ethics. He has a talent for breaking down complex ethical dilemmas into manageable frameworks, a skill that has made him a sought-after speaker and board member. French's ethical leadership approach is moral and practical, informed by years of making high-stakes decisions in competitive business environments.

In addition to his professional accomplishments, French is an accomplished GT racing driver. This pursuit has sharpened his understanding of the importance of split-second decisions and the balance between risk and responsibility lessons he applies to business ethics.

In Proverbs for Profit: Ancient Wisdom for Modern Business Ethics, French draws on his vast experience to bridge the gap between ancient wisdom and modern ethical challenges. Combining timeless principles with contemporary case studies, he offers readers a unique and powerful approach to ethical leadership in the 21st century.